IT'S YOUR MOVIE!

Tune Into Your Channel And Create
The Life of Your Dreams

PATRICIA McHUGH

FriesenPress

Suite 300 – 852 Fort Street
Victoria, BC, Canada V8W 1H8
www.friesenpress.com

Copyright © 2014 by Patricia McHugh
First Edition — 2014

All rights reserved.

No part of this publication may be reproduced in any form, or by any means, electronic or mechanical, including photocopying, recording, or any information browsing, storage, or retrieval system, without permission in writing from the publisher.

ISBN
978-1-4602-5068-6 (Hardcover)
978-1-4602-5069-3 (Paperback)
978-1-4602-5070-9 (eBook)

1. Body, Mind & Spirit, General

Distributed to the trade by The Ingram Book Company

TABLE OF CONTENTS

VII   Intro

1   **SECTION ONE**
My Journey: How I Learned

3   Chapter 1: Where I Started

9   Chapter 2: How I learned

13   Chapter 3: My First Time

17   Chapter 4: A Book...Really?

23   **SECTION TWO**
Through The Channel

25   Chapter 5: About Channels and Channeling

31   Chapter 6: There Are Many Ways to Get Guidance

43   Chapter 7: Who is Anthony?

47   Chapter 8: Who Am I and Why Am I Here?

55 Chapter 9: It's Your Movie!

63 Chapter 10: Your Mind is a Projector

73 SECTION THREE
The Transcripts

75 Chapter 11: About the Transcripts

81 Chapter 12: Week One

119 Chapter 13: Week Two

149 Chapter 14: Week Three

181 Chapter 15: Week Four

215 Chapter 16: Week Five

229 Chapter 17: Week Six

241 Chapter 18: Final Week

245 SECTION FOUR
Where To Next?

247 Chapter 19: Simple Ways to Open a Channel

253 Chapter 20: That's a Wrap!

INTRO

All my life I searched for happiness. In my early years, I did it by trying to run or hide from the things I saw as making me unhappy. When my first child was born I changed to actively seeking, striving and trying to achieve a state of happiness. It worked to a degree. I was a contributing member of society, had the trappings of success and what appeared to be a happy family. I thought I was working toward a secure retirement, a time when I could play golf and relax, but when my career was abruptly interrupted and I actually retired, it wasn't enough. I still didn't feel happy and began searching for something else.

At times I searched for another business to start, saying, "I have one more big thing left in me." But the world of business and politics had lost its luster. There had to be something else. It was well hidden, but I found what I was looking for. It was in another dimension.

At 62 I opened a channel to high-level guide who speaks using my voice. Among the first words spoken were "Call me Anthony." Through the channel, Anthony gave me the keys to creating a happy life. Anthony described my life as a movie where I write the script, play the starring role, and am the entire audience. He helped me to remember who I am, where I came from, and why I am here. He explained how my mind works and how I use emotions to create my life experience. Anthony also explained who 'he' is: *"I am you and you are me and together we are we."*

This is our story.

SECTION ONE

My Journey: How I Learned

CHAPTER 1:
WHERE I STARTED

Had I been born in the 90s or later, I could easily have been labeled ADD. The term didn't exist in my world when I was growing up, so I was labeled "high-strung" by my grandmother, "uncooperative" by my teachers, and "rebellious" by my parents. My school years were a pretty bumpy ride. I was five years old when I started grade one. (Kindergarten didn't exist in those days.) My parents were both teachers, and I didn't have any trouble with the school work. The problem for me was the confinement, both mental and physical. I was bored, and itched to be outside with my two little sisters. By spring, it had become such an ordeal to get me to go along willingly that my parents let me stay home until the end of the school year when I went back to "graduate."

And so it went all through my school years. I resisted, played hooky, and caused no end of grief. I just couldn't focus. A day in the classroom seemed to take forever, and I found it almost impossible to sit still, pay attention, and follow the rules. I didn't really act up that much. I just checked out.

It wasn't until I looked into the eyes of my firstborn and saw the reflection of a commitment made long before that I knew I had to buckle down and become responsible. And I did. I became the model of responsibility. I went to college, studied hard, became an accountant, got a good job and supported my daughter. But I still found it hard to sit still for any length of time. My mind bounced from "I should be doing this" to "I forgot to do that," and my body went along for the ride.

Years later when the movie *The Secret* was first released, my daughter and my sister both suggested I watch it. Watching movies had never been high on my list. I always said, "They take too long, I can't sit still that long." The movie sounded interesting but I was in a cycle of achieving and earning and gave it a pass.

At the time I was deep into the world of business and politics. I had a big title, was on a first-name basis with most of the Cabinet Ministers and the Premier of our Provincial Government, was involved with lawyers and municipal government leaders in the creation of new legislation and was generally flying high . . . or so I thought. And then my world shifted. The resort I was managing was sold and the new owners wanted to manage it themselves.

The next few years were a little shaky for me. Being a female past the mid-century mark in a relatively isolated mountain valley in western Canada during an economic downturn didn't make for the best opportunities to start a new business or find a job similar to the one I had. And quite frankly, I wasn't sure I wanted to. I was seeing the picture through a different lens and I wasn't sure I liked it anymore. So I retired and put on the happy. I spent time with my grandchildren, played golf, drank wine with my friends, and when the sun went down I wondered if this was all there was going to be from here on out.

At the same time, my daughter was exploring the world of spirit guides and angels. We talked on the phone and she would tell me about the books she was reading and the people she was meeting. My mind was being stretched and I gradually started to open more to the realization that I was not just a human being. I was also a spiritual being.

It wasn't like I was a complete spiritual neophyte. During my earlier career years when I was building businesses and attending Rotary meetings, I had been somewhat of a closet self-help junkie. I read book after book on the power of your subconscious mind and could write out affirmations with the best of them. However, as I look back now on those years, what I was really doing was trying to perfect goal setting and goal achieving. I wanted to be totally in charge. I wanted to dream the dream and make it come true, and I wanted to use my conscious mind to direct the power of my subconscious to make it happen.

Things were different now, my world had changed and I was feeling out of control, so when my daughter suggested I make an appointment with one of her new friends, an intuitive counselor ("Come on, Mom. What can it hurt?"), I did. And it didn't hurt. In fact, I rather liked it. You might say I got hooked. And one thing led to another. I bought some Angel cards and learned to give myself daily readings, and I made more intuitive/psychic appointments. The information I got from these sessions was interesting and helpful, but it was kind of like getting a massage. It felt fabulous while it was happening, and I still felt great for a while after, but gradually the comfort and relaxed feeling faded, and the old discomfort came back. Giving myself readings with my Angel cards was fun too, but I was never really sure what the cards were telling me.

I never did watch the movie *The Secret,* but a year or so later I read the book. It was interesting, and from there I somehow found a video of Esther Hicks channeling Abraham. This was my first exposure to channeling, and I remember thinking "How cool is that?" I became fascinated with the whole idea of channeling and with Abraham's message, so I ordered the CDs and listened to them over and over again. When I tired of Abraham, I became enthralled with *A Course in Miracles* scribed by Dr. Helen Schucman. Dr. Shucman describes the experience writing her book as taking dictation from an inner voice that dictated to her on its own schedule.

I followed the *Course in Miracles* religiously every morning for a year. Again, I enjoyed the message, and I was also intrigued with the idea that the book was channeled. Somehow channeled information was of more value to me. It wasn't just some talking head. It was a higher power. It came from "out there" where we couldn't see and where "they" knew a lot more than we did.

By this time my daughter and my granddaughters were talking regularly about their spirit guides and I became more interested. I was in a bookstore one day and came across a book written by Sylvia Browne called *Contacting Your Spirit Guide.* I read the book and by following the visualization exercise instructions in it was able to connect with a guide called Alexander. I communicated with Alexander by asking questions and receiving responses that were sometimes "intuition" and sometimes jolts of energy running through my body. This experience brought me some comfort, but I was never quite sure if it was guided intuition or my ego talking. The "conversations" were also very limited. It was mostly "yes" or "no" responses to questions, and I wanted more. I wanted to learn about things I couldn't imagine. I didn't just want feedback. I wanted expansive guidance so I asked Alexander to talk to me in a way that I could either see or hear but it never happened.

Some time passed. I was still giving myself Angel card readings and had started to journal. We live in Canada and also have a winter home in Arizona. I was in Arizona for the winter playing golf, hiking, and reading. The house is in a gated 55+ retirement community where the major activities are playing golf and having happy hour . . . right up until 7:00 pm when the streets are rolled up and the lights go out. The topics of conversation were generally "What did you shoot today?" "Guess what my grandchildren are doing now?" and the health update. Channeling wasn't on the "open for discussion" list.

My husband was still working and he was back in Canada most of the winter. We talked on the phone every day and the topics were broadened to include the work and stock market update but we didn't venture into spirit guides or channeling. That was in what my husband called flaky territory and we didn't go there.

Not after that lazy weekend morning some months back when the flake label had been brought up. My husband was sitting at the breakfast bar in our kitchen, eating and surfing on his computer. I was lounging in a nearby recliner, reading and musing . . . until his voice broke into my peaceful reverie.

"This flake is saying that . . . "

I don't remember what the "flake" was saying but I do remember feeling my buttons being pushed and my quick response: "FLAKE?"

"Well yeah, you know one of those guys who is not mainstream." He was backpedalling a bit. "You know, like you're a flake." He was smiling now, doing his best "What the hell just happened and how do I rewind?" move.

Being emotionally advanced and feeling somewhat laid back that day, I let it go. But it was still there in the air, and we didn't talk about reincarnation, spirit guides, and angels.

I had lots of time to think in Arizona and was a bit bored so the question of "what is my purpose in this life?" weighed heavy on my mind. One of the psychics I had visited a few years prior had told me all the hard work in this life was done and I was now in a golden phase. She said she didn't see anything more that I needed to do and that I was just to have fun. Sounded good at the time, but we Type As need to see a little more in life. I searched around again for business opportunities but nothing seemed appealing.

TV didn't hold much interest for me and on quiet evenings, I found myself spending more and more time on the Internet listening to blog talk radio and watching YouTube videos— searching for answers to questions I couldn't even put into words.

CHAPTER 2:
HOW I LEARNED

One evening early in 2013, I was cruising through YouTube and landed on a video that showed several people channeling entities that used the human channel's voice. The people who were channeling appeared not to be aware of what was happening at the time and the voices were not the same as their normal speaking voices. Some actually had totally different accents when they were channeling. The channeled messages were very clear and informative but not altogether new territory for me. I had already heard similar things on YouTube videos that used "mechanical" Internet voices. What did grab my attention in that particular video was the mention of a book from which people could learn to channel. The book is *Opening to Channel: How to Connect with Your Guide* by Sanaya Roman and Duane Packer, information at www.orindaben.com.

Now we were talking my language! I immediately ordered the book on my Kindle and began to read. This was what I had been searching for. The authors, Sanaya Roman and Duane Packer, described their own experiences learning to channel high-level guides and they provided step by step directions and guidance on how to do it yourself.

The journey had begun in earnest.

These words from the preface of the book were like music to my ears: "Channeling is a skill that you can learn. To channel, you do not have to be spiritually evolved or have been a psychic all your life; you do need patience, perseverance, and a strong desire to make the connection."

Wow, Sanaya and Duane's book could teach me how to channel and I would be able to do it consciously so that I was aware of what my guide was saying. This was exactly what I was looking for. Sanaya and Duane went on to say they had already taught thousands of people to channel, and as a result, the people's lives were changed for the better. They had more compassion for themselves and others, and many became more prosperous and had a clearer vision of what they were here to do. Yes, yes, and yes!

That night I read until I was too tired to read any more and as soon as I got up the next morning, I started reading again. It seemed I couldn't take it in fast enough. Unless they are novels, I don't often read books straight through from front to back. I usually scan the table of contents and hit the highlights first. That is what I had done with this book.

Opening to Channel: How to Connect with Your Guide is divided into four sections. The first section contains background information on channeling and includes things like—"how it will feel, who the guides are, how guides communicate with you, and how to know if you are ready to channel." I really wanted to know if I was ready, so I read this section first. Sanaya and Duane have a very easy writing style, and in the book they relate accounts of their everyday life and their channeling interactions with their guides Orin and DaBen. They had both been channeling for years. Sanaya had been teaching Earth Life courses channeled by her guide Orin and Duane had been channeling his guide DaBen to assist in his healing work. They had been teaching other people to channel for some time and had now written this book so that more people could learn. Okay, they thought people could learn from a book, so maybe I could.

The second section is laid out as a course for learning to channel. It contains exercises that you can do at your own pace. One line in the description of this section really caught my eye. "Chapter 7, Connecting with Your Guide, and begin verbally channeling in an afternoon." Wow, this wasn't going to take weeks; if I could do the exercises in Chapter 6, I could begin verbally channeling that afternoon. The book also suggested that I record the session so that I could have a record and be able to listen to it again. I didn't have anything to record with so I quickly went online and ordered a little digital recorder from Amazon. It arrived the next afternoon and I was ready to go.

The third section contains stories about how Sanaya and Duane learned to channel and stories about some of their students. The description of that section says, "The stories illustrate some of the common problems people have as they open to channel and include steps you can take if you encounter these problems." I figured it would be good to at least skim through this section before I got down to the serious business of trying to connect with a guide, so I quickly read through the section.

The fourth section is Developing Your Channeling. It contains lots of wonderful information on how to strengthen and get the most of your channel once you have learned to connect. I didn't need that yet. What I needed was to find out if I could actually do this. So I skipped this section for the time being and went back to the second section to give it a try.

CHAPTER 3:

MY FIRST TIME

I had made a sleepy attempt to contact a guide the night before but this was my first structured attempt at opening to channel. I was nervous and excited and was at the stage where I felt that everything had to be set up just so for it to "work."

I can still see myself sitting on a cushion on the floor in my bedroom. The book suggested I find a time and place where I wouldn't be interrupted. This was no problem as I was alone in our house in Arizona; my family was miles away in Canada and I had unplugged the phone. My legs were outstretched, and my back was leaning against the bed supported by a nice comfy pillow. (I am not one of those uber flexible people that has meditated for years and can sit for hours in a lotus position.) I had the microphone that came with my new little digital voice recorder clipped to my shirt. The drapes were closed and all was quiet.

And so it began, relaxing and opening to channel. I turned on the recorder and began following the techniques described in the book to establish a connection with a suitable guide. The book suggested listening to meditation music, and I was listening to the only meditation music I had, a Chakra Meditation I bought online. That lasted only a minute or so before I pulled out my earplugs—the music had some background words and I found this distracting.

I continued to relax and do the breathing exercises Sanaya and Duane described and then also began mentally asking for assistance from Sanaya and Duane's guides, Orin and DaBen, as had been suggested in their book.

The total elapsed time on my recorder for that first channel was twenty-seven minutes. The first 13 of those minutes contained only moaning and breathing sounds. This was the time during which I was communicating mentally with Orin and DaBen and visualizing, following the instructions in the book. At times during these first minutes, the energy was strong, and I was experiencing physical sensations. It was especially strong around my eyes with my eyeballs being pulled up and my eyelids down. This was a bit painful and I was also experiencing some muscle spasms. I was physically uncomfortable and silently asked Orin and DaBen to make it easier. They guided me to relax and breathe and the discomfort subsided.

The book had prepared me for these physical sensations and I understood what was happening. Establishing a channel is a joint effort. I was opening myself to receive information in the form of an energy transmission from another dimension. Our frequencies are different. My guide was searching for a frequency that we could both connect to—similar to tuning in with a radio dial trying to find a channel that will come in clearly.

As had been recommended, I was looking for a high-level guide with whom I felt comfortable. I was looking for the highest frequency and the highest level of information possible. The channel showed me three guides before I found the one I knew was a fit.

The first guide I encountered entered my body and danced it, joyful, playful, really having fun. There was definitely a channel open and we were on the same frequency. I didn't have a visual impression of this guide. It seemed to me to be an enhanced version of my experiences with Alexander. There were only physical sensations. My physical body was rocking and I liked this, but even though it was attractive to me, full of gaiety and playfulness, I felt it wasn't a high enough level of energy, and I wouldn't get clear guidance from it, so I decided to move on to look for a higher level guide.

I asked Odin and DaBen to bring me another, and I tried to describe what I was looking for. "I need a stronger, more intellectual, trustworthy guide that I can rely on and learn from. One that I won't try to dominate, steer, or look after . . . a stronger one."

Next I saw a vague image of an older man, sitting in a big stuffed armchair. He was wearing a brown suit and looked very wise, trustworthy, and intellectually strong. I think he said his name was Orem and I was tempted, but it felt sort of boring, almost like what I would get would be lectures on what had happened in the past and some philosophizing on the future. So I went on looking for a different guide.

I was then shown a visual of a large white door and was guided to go through it. As I opened the door, beautiful rays of light came shining through. Through the light, I could make out what looked like a council of people seated behind a long semi-circle shaped desk. And then, out of the misty light came a big warrior type with armor and a weapon of some sort over his shoulder. Not this one, not a fighter, just strong and someone I can rely on and not have to look after. I am done with weakness. And so we moved on.

Next I felt an energy entering my body, and all I saw was a pinkish wispy image floating in front of me. I liked it, the feel of it, and for some reason it felt right. I asked it to take over my voice and speak to me. Up to this point, all the conversations had been silent.

When the guide started talking with my voice, it was difficult and clumsy. My mouth and lips were moved around and I felt as though I was gagging. When I listen to that first recording now, it sounds pretty crude, but at the time I was so excited that it was actually happening that each sound coming out of my mouth was a triumph. The first words I heard were "Call me Anthony."

The next day I opened the channel again, and Anthony came through, speaking to me using my voice. I was so excited. It wasn't just a fluke thing! We could do this again and again. And we did.

CHAPTER 4:

A BOOK...REALLY?

I was thrilled with my channeling experiences. It was exciting and eye-opening and I couldn't wait to listen to and transcribe the recordings. On the third day, after listening to the recording all the way through twice, I went for a walk. On my walk, Anthony made it clear that he was giving me information to write a book.

Wow, this was no longer just a beautiful solitary personal experience, and I started to worry. As long as I thought the messages were just for me to help me with my earthly journey, I was fascinated. Now we were writing a book, and it was meant to help a lot of people. Would a lot of people be interested in vague and personal messages from Anthony to me? Could we offer a book that was basically a chronicle of these messages? How would that help people?

I expressed my concerns to Anthony that day and he explained to me the purpose of the book. *Tell them the story. Show them that it doesn't have to be perfect, that you don't have to be a psychic medium or a professional channeler to connect with guidance levels. Let them see the messiness and hear the individual and personal way in which we communicate with you so they will be open to trying themselves and being excited by their own unique results. Encourage them to try to contact their own higher level guidance and to receive the loving messages and assistance in their own unique way, through their own unique filter, colored by their own unique life experience. We desperately want to communicate directly with everyone on Earth. Each is a sovereign, powerful, unique being and we are waiting for them to open up to the possibilities so we can work directly with them.*

This made sense to me. It had been relatively easy for me to do something I never dreamed I would be able to do. If I could do it, then anybody else who really wanted to could do it too.

And so we began. Days passed, we channeled and I recorded, transcribed, and made notes. And periodically I worried about how I was actually going to write a book.

It was almost four months after that day when Anthony first told me we would be writing a book and I was again worrying about how to write it. It seemed to be so "I" oriented. It was fascinating to me, but my job was to help you by sharing my experiences in a way that would fascinate you and encourage you to try channeling yourself. "How the hell was I going to do that?" The question dominated most of my waking moments and had even begun to wake me at night.

I felt the urgency to finish the book and knew at some level that it was needed but I didn't see myself as a seer or change leader. Actually, although I accept that some people think I'm a bit flaky, I'm more of a wait and see kind of person. I'm not an "early adopter." I know that because I have an MBA. Early adopter is marketing speak for consumers who are among the first to buy, try, or accept new things. They jump right in with both feet.

I was a teenager in the hippie era but I didn't smoke pot or engage in "free love." I learned to type when it was still typing and not keyboarding. When computers came along, I learned MS-DOS. When Microsoft introduced its revolutionary Windows program, I stuck with DOS. I stuck with DOS until there was no more DOS and then I went kicking and screaming. I hated the look of the new Taurus, the car that influenced the style of automobiles for many years, and I still don't own an iPad or an iPhone.

The truth is I am usually one of the majority, those who wait and see if an idea or product is going to catch on before I buy. But this channeling thing and actually writing a book seemed to be something beyond my control. It seemed like the merest whisper about the subject had sent me headlong into the need to learn.

And now the book . . . how in the hell was I going to write a book and why would people want to buy it? This was my question for Anthony that morning . . . actually it was more of a whining demand now that I think of it.

A: Why do you want to channel? Others are looking for the same thing. You are unique and you are also part of the whole. You may want a red car and your friend may prefer blue, but at your center, that place where you are connected and whole, you want the same things. You want to love and be loved, you want to serve and be served, you want to give and to receive and you want to know where you came from and why you are here.

BINGO! This was exactly why I wanted to channel. I wanted to know where I came from and why I was here.

A: *And we want you to know where you came from and why you are here. Because our job is to help you fulfill your purpose. And by you, you know we mean the big YOU ... all of YOU ... all of the beautiful, unique expressions of creation living in a body on a planet at this time in the history of the Earth. We want you to share your channeling experiences to show others that it can be done. It is time. It is time for all who are searching to connect to a higher source.*

Your world has changed dramatically over the last few decades. From isolated, insular communities communicating over the fence or over telephone lines you now have global connections using computers and satellites. The Information Age has been about easy access to information shared by others ... social media, blogging, YouTube, Internet radio ... your world and your access to it has been growing.

It is now time for new information, information that comes from a higher source. You are the beacons, the nodes. You are the most powerful satellites in the world. We are calling you to open up, to receive our information. Your bodies are being made ready. Your frequencies and those of the Earth are shifting. It is time for you to flip the switch, open the channel, and connect with your source. It is time to fulfill your purpose.

Okay, that answers why and what (questions I didn't ask, by the way.) but HOW? And then the quiet voice came again.

A: *What else did we suggest this morning? ... Read through the transcripts, identify the themes, and wrap them in a story the readers will be able to relate to.*

IT'S YOUR MOVIE!

Oh yeah, that.

It sounded like a lot of work, and I was more hoping for an outline or maybe just dictation. Instead I got another pep talk and a gentle kick in the pants. And so I spent the rest of that day reading through the transcripts and trying to build the story.

As I read the transcripts and my journal notes about the other things that were happening in my life at the time, I was transfixed. It was such an experience of communion, of knowing that I was not only not alone but was being supported and loved and encouraged and guided by some utterly fascinating cosmic force . . . an indescribable feeling, really . . . that kept me going. How fantastic it would be if I could help others to experience this feeling, the comfort, the serenity, the love . . . the numb rear end from sitting on my cheap steno chair staring at my computer. (JUST KIDDING.)

The second time I connected with Anthony he told me, *"You have a job to do and your job is to help people to rewire, to open up, to expand, to lose their fears, to come into their own."* Anthony explained there are many things on Earth that I could do in my "job" and the only thing that mattered was that *"you, you, YOU do it."* He meant ME—not just the part of me that is living in a body on this planet—but ME, the magnificent creative being that was created of and by the one true creative source and is still connected to that source and all of creation.

Writing this book is part of my job. I could not start the job while I was fearful and closed off from what I truly am. It didn't happen overnight. Anthony worked hard. His messages were words and pictures woven through and wrapped around my life experiences. He was talking to the part of me that had lived in the density of 3D for 62 years and had been conditioned to forget who I really was. I had no framework for this kind of communication.

I am certainly not the person you would expect to be learning to channel, let alone writing a book about it. I am an accountant with an MBA for heaven's sake. I am a woman in her 60s who built and saved businesses during the years when women were a rarity in the business world. My father once asked me, "Why do you always end up being the boss?" Over the years, I have been labeled with some of those not so nice terms "we" called women back in those days. The more politically correct said I was a Type A, or hyper, or at the very least driven. My children said I was a know-it-all who was never wrong.

My parents were both teachers and they made sure I was literate. Because they were brilliant themselves, they could also judge pretty harshly. I got a sick stomach every time I handed in a paper at university, and I got a sick stomach when I thought about writing this book.

So why did I write it? It's not like there aren't dozens of books out there on channeling. Why write another one? The simple answer is I started writing because "my guides told me to." Almost every time I connected I was told the same thing: "Write the book!" I resisted, whined, procrastinated, and worried, but Anthony was relentless. He wanted me to write the book for me and he wanted me to write the book for you. And I finished writing the book because it became a labor of love that will all be worth it if my story helps one other person live a happier life.

SECTION TWO

Through The Channel

CHAPTER 5:

ABOUT CHANNELS AND CHANNELING

My grandmother loved words. Her favorite books were dictionaries and she encouraged us to explore the delightful world of words. Grandma liked definitions, and I liked stories. It fascinates me how words and ideas evolve and take on different meanings and shapes as we encounter new experiences and gain new insights and perspectives. My left brain/logical side knew I had to include a description or definition of sorts for channeling and my right brain/creative side resisted the rigidity of a definition. The creation of this book was not a linear process. It did not start with a clear outline and then follow step by step until it was finished. The tussle between my logical side and my creative side produced a more wandering journey and in the process, I found myself putting this chapter in the book but leaving it blank, writing around it until the time felt right. And over that time the definition evolved.

I didn't set out to learn to channel. I was attracted to channeling because of the new information I heard being channeled. It was the messages and not the method that intrigued me at first. The people I watched on YouTube and the accounts I read in books were called channeled messages, so in the beginning I might have defined channeling as "hearing guidance from higher levels." I later learned that some people also refer to the work that mediums do in communicating with those who have died or passed over as channeling. It seemed to me that channeling was receiving messages from an entity or spirit in another dimension or another plane. These entities or spirits of people who have passed on have access to intelligence and information that we do not have and that can help us live our lives.

I had a vague idea of people being "chosen" by beings of higher intelligence as the ones who would hear the messages and disseminate them to others. There was an aura of "specialness" attached to this idea, and I was in some ways attracted to the idea of specialness. Specialness to me indicated a special talent or ability, and I was attracted to the feeling of being special. Initially I was attracted to the messages, and then I became attracted to the idea of being one of the "chosen ones" who were here on Earth to help bring profound messages from on high to the masses.

After watching Esther Hicks channel Abraham, I realized the channeled communication could go two ways. In the videos, Abraham would present a message through Esther and then there would be an opportunity for members of the audience to ask questions of Abraham which would be answered through Esther. This was more than just a message to the masses, but for me it still had quite an aura of "specialness" attached. My definition expanded to include: a person who is "channeling" can not only receive information at the will of a higher communicator but can also ask questions and receive direct answers.

My personal experience channeling Anthony changed my

"definition" of channeling, and I began to see it as tuning in to a wavelength or frequency through which your guidance levels, including YOU, the part of you that is not resident in your 3D body, can send and receive information. The information is not merely words you hear with your physical ears or energy or visions you see with your physical eyes. It can be those things, but it is also something more, something not quite describable. As Anthony is fond of saying *"There are no word symbols to describe it,"* but here goes:

When I think of channeling now, pictures and little vignettes appear in my head. I see someone tuning into a radio station with a dial. I see a cell phone conversation. I see water being channeled through a stream or a garden hose and I also see the rapture on the face of a guitar player who sits with eyes closed listening to the beautiful sound he is creating. The waves of sound emanating from the strings of his guitar resonate with parts of him in a way that creates a joyful communion. The sound resonates with more than just the little bones and other physical mechanisms in the guitar player's ears. The music touches him on another level. He feels it in a space that is bigger than the physical confines of his body. There is a communication between the guitar and the player.

This is perhaps the closest I can come to describing what channeling is for me. It is a communion between my higher levels and "me." I am hearing the sounds my higher levels are creating. We are in resonance and I am hearing the language of home.

For me, channeling is more than communicating. It is a profound experience. Imagine how much easier it would have been in school if we had "living" textbooks that not only provided information but loved interacting with us and could sense our level of understanding and adjust the content to suit our unique learning experience. This is what I found when I opened my channel.

In other species and dimensions, beings communicate telepathically. Many of you likely do this to some extent with those closest to you. Parents are often so tuned in to their children they can sense what is happening even when they can't physically see or hear them. Couples who have lived together for many years can finish each other's sentences or answer questions before they are asked. Children growing up in the same house often have these same connections. These people feel more connected and less separate from each other than they do from the rest of the world. They are willing to share wavelengths and unconsciously use them for communication. Your guidance levels are always on your wavelength. If you pay attention, you can sense them. They are communicating with you constantly.

It's not about luck or specialness. I now know that channeling is not about specialness. Each one of us has a channel. When we are born, our channel is open. It is like an umbilical cord to God or the Universe or Creator—whatever you want to call the one source from which and by which everything was created. WE are energetic beings and our energy or essence flows through this cord. WE continue to flow through this umbilical cord (what I call the channel) communicating with our physical bodies and creating our life experience. WE do not just flow into the body until we are all there and then begin our life experience. WE are never "all there" (some of us less so than others). WE continue to communicate and to flow.

Most of us don't know about the channel because we have blocked it. We create a blockage or clog in the channel by resisting the flow. Anthony likens it to resistance in an electrical current or a kink or closed valve in a water hose. As we "grow up" or move through our life experience, the channel becomes more and more clogged.

We are conditioned from birth, and as we try to find our way in the Earth game, we assume roles and identities that help us monitor our progress and keep us safe while we play the game. I think we allow this to happen because we are looking for approval outside of ourselves. It might even be instinctive. Perhaps it is part of the game. We are physically vulnerable and reliant on others to support us for many years. This makes us easy to condition. Some say it needed to be that way because Earth life was a dangerous game. Whatever or however, our channel becomes blocked because we forget who we really are and we put more and more of our energies into supporting the roles and identities we have assumed. We become very adept at seeking outside approval, measuring our worth, and monitoring our world. We learn to judge and assess, we build up our resistance, and resistance blocks the channel.

We came into this world knowing the language of "home" but because we closed off the connection and could no longer hear it, we forgot our mother tongue and learned the 3D language of the Earth game. The beauty of it is the connection is still there and we can reopen it and remember our mother tongue. All it takes is the will to do it.

CHAPTER 6:
THERE ARE MANY WAYS TO GET GUIDANCE

There are many ways to get professional guidance and communication from our higher levels. I used some and I also read books, listened to speakers, and worked with coaches. They each contributed to my journey. Anthony was able to tie all those experiences together and fill in the blanks. They are integral parts of my story. The people I saw and worked with were sharing their talents and gifts. They were doing the job they came here to do and I appreciate them and the part they played in my journey.

In fact, I still consult with intuitives, readers and other teachers. Our higher levels are happy to use any conduit they can to communicate with us. They really want us to open up our own channel and hear the truth of who we are so they can help us live a happy fulfilling life; and, because they will do whatever it takes to get through, our higher selves will give us guidance through another's channel when they can't get through on ours.

Professional Psychics, Intuitive Counselors

It was difficult for me to think of a heading or name for this type of professional guidance. "Professional psychics" doesn't necessarily describe my experiences. If you Google professional psychics, you will find hundreds of people who are "qualified" and "certified" and standing by ready to give you psychic guidance. I have no doubt most of these people are able to connect to guidance levels and provide information you can use in your life experience, but this is not how I experienced professional psychic assistance. I did not Google professional psychics or look in the phone book. I used the largest marketing tool there is—word of mouth.

My first experience was with Tara Taylor, the intuitive counselor my daughter Penny suggested. Penny was referred to Tara by a friend and was very happy with the intuitive counseling she received. Tara was quite busy, but I was able to get an appointment with her because I am Penny's mom.

Being Penny's mom also has advantages when I want to get a last-minute appointment for a pedicure. Mothers seem to have a way of convincing themselves their children are just a little bit easier to love, and after the first couple of times I encountered the special "Ah ... Penny's mom" treatment, I looked at my daughter lovingly. "They must really like you." My daughter laughed. "No, Mom, it's all in the tips."

Anyway, being Penny's mom got me in to see Tara, and she connected with my guides who told her things about my present life and also my probable future that were accurate and helpful. One of the things Tara relayed to me was something big, something that would definitely rock my world. She told me my health was good but my husband's was not. She said I would outlive him and he would pass within five years.

Approximately a year and a half after my first appointment with Tara, I visited another "psychic" whose name is Pat. We were having dinner with a good friend and her family. My friend's son and daughter-in-law were announcing the happy news that they were going to have a baby. This couple had been trying for some time and they were overjoyed. Sometime during that evening, conversation turned to the psychic who had told them not to worry, they would be pregnant soon. The couple had been considering a fertility clinic and the psychic told them there would be no need. My ears perked up and so did those of my sister and my friend. We got the information and contacted Pat to arrange an appointment.

Pat did not advertise. She booked through referrals. I called her office where I received a voice message saying she was very busy, please leave a message, and if requesting an appointment, please also leave the name of the person who referred you. The next day Pat called back and we arranged appointments for my sister, my friend, and me.

Pat's method was slightly different from Tara's. Tara used Angel Cards briefly at the beginning of our session and then she was channeling my guides and relaying their messages to me. Pat did her session mostly by shuffling, laying out and reading a huge deck of tarot cards. She seemed also to be connecting with people who had passed away. My grandmother was mentioned and she passed on some advice that did sound like something my grandmother would say.

Pat's messages were similar to Tara's in many ways and different in some. Like Tara, Pat gave me a very clear message that my husband's health was not good and he would not live much longer. My first appointment with Tara was in January of 2010, and my husband passed away in August of 2013. I had learned to channel before my husband's passing, and my own guides confirmed what would happen.

Although I had "advanced notice" of my husband's passing, I was not given any specifics. It was clear to me that he was in pain much of the time, but he was such a strong man I couldn't quite accept that he would die. He suffered from Crohn's disease, but had not been diagnosed with anything life threatening or terminal, and he worked up until the day, one week before he died, that he just couldn't do it anymore. I was out that morning, and when I came home just after lunch, my husband was home from work and in bed. Coming home from work this early in the day and going to bed was totally out of character and I knew something serious was happening.

Because he had tried to see him a week or so before, I knew my husband's local doctor was away for a month, and when I phoned his Crohn's specialist, I learned he was also away. I was desperate and asked the specialist's receptionist what I should do. She advised me to get him to the emergency room at the regional hospital. I wanted to call an ambulance but my husband refused, so he got in the car and I drove him to the regional hospital an hour away.

He was admitted to that hospital and three days later was taken by air ambulance to a major hospital in Calgary, Alberta, where despite heroic efforts on his part and on the part of a team of doctors and nurses in the intensive care unit, his body gave up, and he passed.

IT'S YOUR MOVIE!

The doctors told us it was a very aggressive form of lymphoma that took his life but I believe it was his decision. It was devastating for those of us still living, but HE had decided that leaving his body and returning "home" was the best thing for him.

Because I had been forewarned and had learned to channel my higher levels, I was able to accept my husband's death on a mental and spiritual level. I could "see" him in a better place. It still hurt terribly, and I suffered both physically and emotionally, but I knew there was more for me to do and that somehow I would have to pull myself together and do it.

One morning after the funeral was over, I was alone in my house. I sat in my chair and gazed out the window wondering what to do and where to go next. I had no motivation to write and I just wanted to go to sleep. I was appealing to Anthony for some guidance, some help. As the sun came up over the Rocky Mountains and lit up the trees in Brewer's pass, I heard these words: *"You couldn't have predicted how it happened with your husband, and you can't predict what will happen now. Just know that it will be beautiful and you will like it. You can't see it from where you are. Just keep moving, and as you go farther you will see farther. And ... since you like practical things, we'll give you something practical to do. Clean out your cupboards."*

I laughed and thought, "Well, you asked for guidance, and this is what you got!" so I stood up and started cleaning out the cupboards. I spent two full days cleaning out cupboards, and then I tackled the biggest mess of all: my office. It wasn't a cure, but I definitely felt better, lighter somehow. I began to put one foot in front of the other, and gradually the words started to flow again.

Grieving is a process and it certainly wasn't over. I was not happy with myself and would tell myself, "Get your shit together and get on with it!" My body still felt shaky and I cried a lot. My children were a big help. They packed up his clothes and personal items and took them away, and they visited and helped me through the things like going to the local grocery store for the first time and canceling his cell phone.

Still today, almost four months later, the tears are streaming down my face as I write these words, and I am wondering why I am even writing them. But I know why: I am writing these painful words to try and get across to you that life experiences are not always joyful, but they can be made easier by connecting with our source and remembering who we really are.

There is no doubt in my mind that without the advance notice my higher levels provided and without the loving assistance they continue to provide, my husband's death would have been much harder to accept. Because of Anthony's channeled messages, I did not resist what was or rail against what had happened or demand to know why. I accepted and am doing my best to move on. My soul is at peace. My body and nervous system are still in shock, but my soul is at peace.

Hypnosis

On January 3, 2013 I was cruising through YouTube and landed on a video of an interview with a hypnotherapist named Dolores Cannon. Dolores works with a unique type of hypnosis she has developed over 45 years of using hypnosis to regress people to past lives. She calls her technique Quantum Healing Hypnosis Therapy (QHHT).

In the interview, Dolores talked about the things she has learned over all these years from her clients and her conversations with what she calls her clients' "subconscious." It was fascinating and I wanted to know more about what Dolores was doing. In the interview, it was mentioned that Dolores had written 17 books about her QHHT experiences and I got out my Kindle and ordered one that night. The book was called *Convoluted Universe: Book Four*. It contains stories of different clients, the past lives they experienced and what Dolores learned talking to her clients' subconscious.

I wanted to know more, and when I looked at Dolores' website the next day I found she was teaching others QHHT, and that an on-line version of the Level 1 course was almost ready to be released. I enrolled in the on-line course and completed it on January 31st.

What I read in our QHHT class materials and what I heard Dolores saying on videos and in other YouTube interviews gave me the answer to why I found QHHT so intriguing. Although Dolores said she did not know how to channel or talk to "them," this was exactly what I saw her doing. It's those "word symbol" things again. I say, "channeling your higher self or YOU" and Dolores says, "What makes my technique different and unique from other hypnosis techniques is that I have found a way to go directly to the Source of All Knowledge."

Dolores says she calls it the "subconscious" because she doesn't know what else to call it. She does not mean the subconscious mind in the way that psychiatrists define it because as she says, "That is a childish part of the mind and is the part used by hypnotists to work on habits." Dolores also says that if she had to define it, she would call it the Higher Self or Higher Consciousness or Oversoul, and that the SC (or "they" as she also calls them) have told her they don't care what she calls them.

When a practitioner performs QHHT s/he hypnotizes the client into a somnambulistic state and asks the client's higher levels (SC as Dolores calls it) to show them an appropriate past life where the client can get information that will help them in this life. The practitioner questions the client about what s/he is seeing and the entire session is recorded. After the client has finished viewing the past life and has seen how it ended, the practitioner asks to speak directly to the client's SC. The practitioner then questions the SC to find out what it was in the past life that they chose to show the client that was of value to the client. The practitioner also communicates with the SC to see if s/he can get further messages for the client and also to request a scan of the client's body and ask for healing where appropriate.

I have been regressed twice by a QHHT practitioner and my memories of what I saw and heard, combined with the recordings, provide valuable insight for me in the same way that my recorded and transcribed channel sessions with Anthony do.

At the end of April 2013, I traveled to Arkansas to complete the Level Two QHHT course. At that course, I met other trained QHHT practitioners from around the world. Many of us still keep in touch and I am amazed by their stories and their experiences. My own experiences using Dolores' QHHT technique further convinced me that I was helping people tune in to their own channel and hear messages spoken by their higher levels using their voice. Sound familiar?

Akashic Records

Just after I arrived home from Arkansas, my daughter told me the mother of one of her friends was completing her certification as an Akashic Reader. My daughter said her friend's mom was doing free readings for family and friends as part of her practical course work and asked if I would be interested. I didn't really know much about the Akash and what Akashic Readers do, but was open to find out, so I said "sure," and Penny made an e-introduction.

We scheduled a telephone session and the Reader, Karen Adams, www.akashicjourney.com, asked me to email her some questions ahead of time in case she had time to do some advance reading in my Records. I had vague ideas about the Akash, but I wanted to be more informed before the call, so I did a little research. What I learned is that the Akash is a galactic cyber record of every life that has ever been lived and everything that has ever happened. (This is my paraphrased description.) I sent Karen some questions and was eager to hear what she had to say.

The session was both enjoyable and intriguing. Karen told me she was also an intuitive so she would be reading relevant information in the records and getting information from my guides, relatives who have passed, and other teachers. This sounded familiar and the information/guidance I received from Karen was similar in many ways to what I had heard from psychic counselors and through my QHHT sessions. And again, Karen's information had bits that were different and perhaps colored in some way by her own unique life experiences and filters. I enjoyed the session and found it valuable enough to do it again.

Shortly after my first session with Karen, I signed up for a free on-line tele-summit that was composed of a variety of interviews with different spiritual leaders, teachers and authors. The first interview I listened to was with Lisa Barnett. Lisa is an Akashic Reader who also teaches people how to open and read the Records. As a bonus for telesummit participants, Lisa offered recorded videos of her Level 1 course for 10% of the tuition for the original live course. Sign me up!

I registered and downloaded the workbook and videos and got to work learning how to open and read my own Akashic Records. Following the course manual and Lisa's recorded audio instructions, I would open my Records, ask questions, and write down the answers I received.

One day I was talking with Karen Adams about my experiences learning and opening my Akashic records and she enthusiastically offered to help me. As we talked, she mentioned that the way I was describing my experiences in the Records and what she experienced were quite different. This was my first clue.

I didn't really care what was happening. All I knew was when I followed the process and asked questions, I saw pictures and wrote words. It was like my pen had a mind of its own. The same arthritic fingers I had asked Anthony to heal in one of our early channel sessions held the pen with ease and flew across the page, creating beautiful words. My handwriting had never been this good. I was learning and having fun.

On July 11, 2013 I followed Lisa's process and opened my Records. It was my habit to start by asking this question: "What is the best use of the Akashic Records for me today?" This is what I wrote. *Clarity – you are beginning to see things more clearly. Judgment is falling away and you are moving toward acceptance. The records can answer questions, satisfy curiosity, and reinforce what you already know. You know it. It is in your DNA. The records are like Google and Wikipedia. They shine the light on a way forward you have already walked. The connection is good. It boosts your clarity. You are not being shown, you are remembering. Funny word – because it is all happening at once – but the best word for "today."*

Whoa ... this didn't seem like information from the records, but it did sound very familiar, so my next question was this: "Am I speaking with Anthony?"

A: Yes, and the council. We are helping with this part of your journey as we do with all of your journey. There are more involved here. More energy is being poured into the channel to assist you to see farther with each step. It is all helping—the Akashic Records, the hypnosis, the teachers—and it can be distracting. You do not judge what we say. You accept and open for more. What other Earth beings say is more apt to be judged, measured, or ignored.

You have many balls in the air. All those coaches, advisors, and leaders. They do provide pieces—not actually provide—but help to illuminate. They are there, the pieces, and the others help us to shine enough light that you can see them with clarity. The other side—the flip side of the coin—is that their light comes with attachments that can dampen the energy.

You don't need them. We don't need them.

Now that it is recognized, we can discuss the inkling you had when you first learned to connect. The level of clarity with which you can connect— same thing as vibrational level and frequency—determines the "level" of information you can receive.

First we appeared as Alexander. You could "see" and accept that physical form. You had less resistance to it and could therefore have the most clarity—the clearest connection—the least static. We tried the female form also but you resonated best with the male form in the view that we presented.

When you searched for a "higher-level" guide we presented different images and sensations to see which would be best accepted/cause the least resistance, and that is what we used ... no physicality and warm loving energy.

Now you know it is shape-shifting in a way. Turning the dial—finding the most clear connection. Which one looks better, 1 or 2, 2 or 1? (Anthony was showing me a little video of a person sitting in an optometrist's chair, being asked by the optometrist to choose which was better as he flipped through the different lenses.)

Having names is part of the "specialness" game. The energies communicating are not always the same but they are always in consort with the greater YOU. We cannot entirely describe this with Earth word symbols and there is no need. Suffice to say that we are assisting you to discover that which you already know.

And so there it was. ALL ROADS SEEMED TO LEAD TO HOME.

CHAPTER 7:
WHO IS ANTHONY?

Some of the first words spoken through the channel were *Call me Anthony.* Unlike the first "options" I saw when asking to be connected to a higher-level guide, there was no picture of a man. There was the wispy pinkish somewhat parallelogram-shaped energy floating in my mind. There was the energy entering my body and speaking with my voice, and there was a feeling of love.

Because in my experience the name Anthony is associated with a male person, I refer to Anthony as he. Anthony is not really a he. Anthony closed that first channel session by saying *I am you, and you are me, and together we are we.* I think Anthony gave me a relatively easy and recognizable name to call him because he knew it would be help me in the beginning. It might happen quicker for other people, but I am quite linear, and although I liked the sound of his words *I am you, and you are me, and together we are we,* it took awhile before I was able to get it clear. What I heard was more like, "We are a team." I was still looking for "higher" guidance from someone or something more learned. I heard it, but I wasn't ready to accept it.

Anthony also refers to "we" as in "*We want you to . . .*" and he talks about his "council." On that first day, when I asked to be connected to a higher-level guide and was shown a series of "options," I saw this council. It was a group of people (although it was not a clear picture, they reminded me of older men) seated at a semi-circular table. I got the sense of a group of learned men that provided guidance.

At the time, I was still looking for love in all the wrong places, and the whole package appealed to me. The lack of a physical appearance, the wispy pink energy, the feeling of love and the idea of a backup council of learned old men. This should be a good enough team to give me the guidance I was looking for. And it was. It was perfect. It made me comfortable enough to allow the full weight of Anthony's message *I am you and you are me and together we are we* to sink in.

Anthony helped me to release my fears and feel safe without the boundaries and structure that came with the roles and identities I had assumed in an attempt to be loved, protected, and safe in the unsafe world I thought was my home. Anthony gave me the keys and the power to step up and unlock the door that separated my world from his. Anthony's world is safe and it is also my home.

I am having a blast exploring the new world that has been opened up for me. It isn't entirely clear yet, and maybe it will never be, but one thing is sure: the more I look, the more I see. As Anthony so often says to me, *Just keep moving, and as you go farther you will see farther. Just go! You can't see there from here. Just go!*

I have such a feeling of love when Anthony speaks to me. There is no doubt "he" loves me wholeheartedly and unconditionally. Anthony loves me in the way that only someone who does not have a separate identity to protect can love. Anthony plays no other role. We are not only connected—we are WE and WE are ME.

CHAPTER 8:
WHO AM I AND WHY AM I HERE?

Who am I?

Prior to embarking on this channeling journey, I had read Dr. Bruce Lipton's book *Biology of Belief* and heard several of Jennifer Hough's Wide Awakening messages where she talks about telomeres and cellular communication. I had also read William Linville's book *Living in a Body on a Planet*.

My daughter, bless her gifted beautiful soul, had by this time introduced me to the idea of souls, multiple lives, soul family groups, and soul clusters. She encouraged me to read a book called *Many Lives, Many Masters* written by a prominent psychiatrist named Brian Weiss. The book is an account of Dr. Weiss' experience with one of his patients as they explored her past lives. I found the book very interesting and it had the ring of truth for me.

Perhaps the most valuable part of that experience was that it led to many wonderful conversations with my daughter about how we chose to be together in this life and had done so in many previous lives. And, thank you . . . thank you . . . thank you . . . my daughter came to realize that she chose everything about this life, including her name. She would never again look accusingly at me with those flashing brown eyes and say, "Why did you have to give me such a stupid name?"

Suffice to say that I was quite settled with the idea that I am a spiritual being having a life experience on Earth. That I was settled with the idea didn't mean I was comfortable with it or that I had embodied it. It was an idea I accepted as being valid. I had seen enough evidence to accept the conclusion.

The simple fact that I was still searching, asking for guidance through others or through a channel from a "higher-level guide," was enough to show me that I had not quite accepted the idea as truth. It took hearing the words directly from the source before I was fully able to accept the truth of who I am.

I am living a human experience and the human part of me wants to hear it with my own ears or see it with my eyes. I like logical, scientific evidence and I want proof. It's how most of us roll as humans. Yes, I had contacted my guides, had meditated and "seen" them, and could feel their presence and sense their message; I had paid for and received good advice and assistance from people with advanced psychic and intuitive abilities, but I wanted solid evidence. I wanted proof, and what constituted proof for me was "hearing it with my own ears." My guidance realms were ready. And when I was ready, it truly was as simple as allowing it to happen, opening my end of the channel.

IT'S YOUR MOVIE!

My logical side was fascinated with scientific theories and explanations of things like quantum physics, fractals, and black holes. I tried very hard to grasp the entirety of these concepts and often fell short of the mark. I was looking for proof, trying to see the "whole big picture." Anthony taught me that striving to understand and "get it" interferes with the channel. Not only does it not help, it hinders. Going around in circles trying to figure things out and be in charge means I will see the same scenery over and over.

In our very first channeled message, Anthony told me I was him and he was me. Here was proof. I was not just this little person in a body. I was also "out there" somewhere.

In our second channel, Anthony told me he would take away all my fears; I no longer needed them. He told me I was *"strong, powerful, magnificent, and beyond, far beyond the reach of physical harm."* He also said, *"You know who you are. You are one with the one. And there is no need at all for you to be afraid of anything at all in this physical plane because there is nothing, Nothing, NOTHING at all that can hurt you."*

It was thrilling, it truly was. Hearing the words come out of my mouth, seeing the little videos playing on the screen in my mind, feeling the physical sensations and the love flowing through was freakin' awesome. Here was the proof I needed. There really is a Dog. (Sorry, old joke.) Seriously though, this was a life-changing experience. It gradually quieted my fears and made room for peace to creep into my soul.

In writing this chapter, I came to fully appreciate Anthony's rambling messages and frustration over trying to use words to describe something for which there are no words. I will do my best to "language" the truth about who I am as I know it today. I have learned that truth is a moving target and that as I go farther, I will see farther.

The entirety of who I am is not clear to me at this time. In describing who I am, I also need to describe who you are. Please know that this is my truth and does not have to be accepted by you.

Here we go ... I was created of and by the one true creative source. I was individuated as a unique piece of creation and I am an incarnation of the creator. I am unique but not separate. Since I am not separate from all that is I am ~~not~~ connected to all that is. I am separate only in the sense that I can be identified. I am not better than or less than any other piece of creation. Since I am an incarnation of the original creative source I cannot be destroyed or re-created.

From a 3D Earth plane perspective, I am the "being" part of the human being my family and friends know as me. My Earth parents were involved in the creation and nurture of my body and I provided the spark that gave it life. My body is my partner. I cannot function on this plane without it. Its DNA holds the records of all my previous lives and everything I learned in 3D. My body is a highly-advanced robotic device powered and operated by me. Its cells contain receivers and they receive MY power and instructions.

This creeps very close to a topic that goes beyond the scope of this book. It is a topic that can generate an emotional reaction similar to religion and politics. It is the topic of sickness and disease. We will not go there today. That I gave my body life also means to me that it is I who will choose to remove the life force. My body will not get sick or wear out and die at which time "I" will leave the body and go somewhere else. Rather I will withdraw the life force from my body, stop the flow of energy, and my body will "die" in a way that is similar to how a battery loses its charge. This is part of a much bigger conversation with Anthony about power and energy, and we will not go there today either.

My "being" also created a mind and a different type of body, an emotional body. My mind and emotions and how I use them in the creation of my life experience are in another chapter.

Why am I Here?

In my spiritual journey, I have learned and unlearned some things about why I am here living a life on Earth. I learned that we incarnate to complete lessons from previous lives or to learn new lessons. I had visions of a checklist with all the lessons on it, and with each life you chose some lessons and then set out to work on them. I also learned about something called Karma and that because of it you were required to work on righting wrongs you had done to another in a previous life. This never really sat well with me. It all conjured up images of school and hierarchies and moving through the grades until you graduated, and then maybe you got to be an angel who didn't have to come to Earth anymore. All in all, I was not entirely comfortable with the scenario.

Because he knew it was one of the things that was really important to me and that the answer would provide a key to the happy life I was searching for, Anthony opened the subject the second day we channeled. He told me I came here with a job to do. I am to be of assistance in helping others open up to the truth of who they really are. He says I don't have to do anything special other than be ME. On another occasion, he told me I was here to be and be seen. I understood this to mean that I was to find the truth of who I am, be it, and let others see me being it.

Three weeks later, Anthony told me that the bigger ME is creating the experiences for me. There is no outside expectation or approval required. Here are some of his words.

A: There is no expectation of you. There is no plan, no group of spirit people gathering around conferencing on how well you're doing with the plan. You are much more powerful than that! You are not a little rat we put in a maze to watch how you run around and get through it. NO. You are you and I am you and together we are creators, crea-tor, crea-tion. You are not a toy. You are not a hope or a wish that was sent out from on high to perform some magic on a plane that was taking a nosedive. NO. That is not what you are! You are magnificent creation. You are pre-approved!

Anthony was not finished with this one. It was important. He came back to it later and added, *There is no need to fix or guide or prod or poke. Our communication, our messages are you talking to you. They do not come from us to you to guide you in the way a dog trained to do so will guide a person with limited physical sight.*

I fell in love with the idea that I was not being judged and I didn't have to figure out what the grand plan was for this life. The big ME was in charge and I didn't have to worry about it. There were no lessons to be learned, and I wasn't being graded or measured. Knowing this gave me the peace of mind I needed to relax and open up to the life the big ME was creating.

IT'S YOUR MOVIE!

Knowing that I am much more than I can possibly see or even comprehend has taken away my feelings of loneliness and vulnerability. I no longer need anyone or anything to make me feel safe, and I am never alone.

When I was in my mid-thirties, an age at which people usually consider themselves adults, I was out on a very large lake in Northern Saskatchewan in a wooden motorboat. My husband, who was the same age, was running the boat. The wind had come up and the water was rough. It was almost dark and we couldn't yet see the shore. I was uncomfortable, and I wanted my Uncle Ivan. Uncle Ivan was my mother's uncle. Her father had been killed in a farm accident when she was only two years old and Uncle Ivan, one of her father's brothers, had been my mother's surrogate father and my surrogate grandfather. As a kid, I spent many happy summers on the farm dogging after Uncle Ivan and "helping" him run things. I always felt safe with Uncle Ivan.

As we crashed through the waves, wind whipping our jackets and water spraying in our faces, I looked at my husband and wondered, *When will we be old enough to be the adults?* As a child, I wasn't worried about being afraid. All kids were afraid sometimes, weren't they? But in my child-mind, Uncle Ivan was all grown up and he wasn't afraid. I wanted to be all grown up.

I don't need my Uncle Ivan anymore because, thanks to Anthony, I now have ME.

CHAPTER 9:
IT'S YOUR MOVIE!

In our formal sessions, Anthony often said, "It's your movie! Write it the way you want to see it." The transcripts contain many references to this metaphor and the messages often include directions to write the screenplay and leave the details to THEM. Anthony used images and words to describe my life as scenes I was creating on a big white screen in my mind. Anthony told me my life was my movie and I was watching the movie of my life in a theater called Earth. I created the movie, I am the star, and I am the sole member of the audience.

I liked this idea and it was entertaining, but when I tried to understand it my head hurt. I was good with me being the sole creator of my movie and also with me being the star. It didn't even bother me that I was the only one in the audience. *Independence* is my middle name and what other people think of me is not a big concern. So it was all good—except for the other people. I could grasp the part about bit actors, the people who just filled in the crowds but how would I deal with the closer ones—my family, friends, neighbors, co-workers, and all those I would need in order to make the movie

I wanted. How could I make sure the props would appear when I wanted them? How could I just write a script and be sure everybody would follow it? How could I make them do what I wanted them to do so I could have the life of my dreams?

Anthony could sense this confusion and he came at it from a different angle: **IT'S THEIR MOVIE!** He hit me where it would hurt the most—my children, because I desperately wanted my children to be happy. I got quite anxious when I saw them headed down what I perceived to be an unhappy path. Anthony provided valuable guidance and assistance with this often gut-wrenching problem.

I had accepted who I really was and by extension who they really were. When all was well and their lives seemed to be running smoothly, it was easy for me to see my children as unique, powerful, and creative beings. When they were happy I was comfortable with that.

Nonetheless, the pull of an unhappy child is a very strong one. One night I was worried about one of my children and couldn't sort out in my mind whether I should step in and help or watch hopefully from the sidelines. It was a long and uneasy night for me. By the time I sat down to channel the next morning, I had convinced myself that I could detach from the "problem," but I was uneasy and I was still worried.

Anthony helped me to see that I had blurred the lines between my movie and my child's. Instead of creating and watching my movie, I was fully involved in watching his and I was trying to figure out how to help him rewrite the parts I was seeing as undesirable.

IT'S YOUR MOVIE!

Here is some of what Anthony had to say that day:

A: You think you're relaxed because you are sitting, but you're wound up. Your head is focused. It's focused on fixing ... fixing again. "What can I do to help? Why don't they pay attention to me?" Fixing ... fixing.

They're not broken. They don't need fixing. They are creating. They are creating a movie that they don't like ... that they don't want to watch, that it's hard for them to watch. It makes them feel bad, but it's their movie. It's their movie! You are not the caretaker. You are not the caretaker. And they are not asking for you to play a role.

If you go into the movie theaters of your children, you will not recognize the movie. They are the movies of their lives as they are seeing them. You cannot write their movies. You can write their parts in your movie and you can see them in your movie the way you want to see them. They might not recognize themselves if they came into your theater and saw them in your movie ... they won't. But it's your movie. Write them how you want them to be in your movie! You want them to be happy; write that. See that! Watch it play on that big beautiful screen. See it! That's all you can do. That's all you can do. That's all there is. That's all you have dominion over. Your movie, your creation, your life.

Stay in your own theater! It's not your job to help them write their movies. They don't need your help writing their movies. It's not your job. Your job is to create your life ... to create what you want.

But I didn't want to feel bad. In my movie I only wanted to feel good. If my children are unhappy, will it make me feel bad? Yes, in all likelihood it will. Me thinking positive thoughts will not change how they feel. Me pretending I don't feel bad will not change how they feel, and it won't make me feel good. Anthony helped me to see that where I stepped out of my movie and into theirs was when I let my feeling bad trigger my need to fix it. In Anthony's lingo, I would then be trying to write their script.

But I couldn't see it. If I stayed in my own theater and let them write their own script, how was I going to keep myself from feeling bad? I couldn't just say, "I am going to write my children as happy, loving, and lovable people. Okay, higher levels—over to you. Make them be that way in my movie. I know I can't change how they are in their own movie, but in my movie I want them to be mature, loving, conscientious, responsible, and happy."

That is not what Anthony meant. What he was telling me was to change the way I see them. I couldn't change the way my children behaved, the actual things they did, but I could certainly change the way I saw them. This is what Anthony was telling me to do. Change the way your children appear in your movie.

It was not the things my children did and said that caused me sleepless nights or stomach upset. It was how I "saw" them. When I "saw" them as lost, unhappy kids who needed fixing, my body responded with the appropriate emotions, and in so doing, created an act and scenes in my movie called, "I am the mother of a lost, unhappy child whose behavior is causing me to be upset." And that is how I would see myself.

There were times when all seemed to be going well with my children, but something else in my life seemed to be making me feel bad. Acting as if what was happening wasn't happening or affirming that I now felt good didn't seem to work. I still felt bad. And

IT'S YOUR MOVIE!

where I really got myself into trouble was when I decided there was nothing I could do about feeling bad because the cause was out of my control someone else should fix it or DO SOMETHING! This is what Anthony describes as, "handing out pens and letting other people write the script for me." As he so kindly told me, "They don't even want to."

The lights were coming on but I still wasn't home. So Anthony had another go at it. I'm paraphrasing here: "You don't just write the script, send it in, and then sit down and watch the entire movie of your life play out. It is an experience you create as you watch. It's the time thing that has you again. It all happens at the same time: you create, you watch, you re-create, you watch. It is a living movie. It's also a control thing. You think you need to write the script in advance get it all sorted out and know what is going to happen so you can sit back and relax and enjoy the movie.

"Not so. When you write the script in too much detail and too far in advance you become attached to it. You are attached to outcomes, and when things don't play out in real life the way you wrote them, when the props don't appear or the supporting actors mess up their lines, you re-act. You don't act like the happy, fulfilled person you created in your script. It can't work! This is why you are having such trouble with the message."

A: Undo the attachments. It's the attachments that create the worry, the angst. It's the attachments that cause the resistance. It's the resistance that lowers the energy and produces the emotions that bounce back and provide experiences that are not what you want or not what you think you want.

One part I kept missing was this: you can only write the script for you. Anthony brought this topic up many times and in many different ways: "*You write the script and we will provide the supporting actors.*" "*You can't see there from here. Just keep going and as you go farther you will see farther.*" "*Just go with the flow.*" "*You don't have to be the director or producer.*"

Just sit in that seat. Put your feet up on the back of the seat in front of you. It's your theater. You can do whatever you want. Have a drink, have some snacks, and enjoy it . . . just enjoy it! Feel it, hear it, smell it, sense it, enjoy it. It's your movie. It's your movie.

It is not your job to build the props, to find the extras and the supporting actors and train them and supervise them and feed them donuts and make sure they're happy, that their trailers are good, that everybody gets along, that they do what they're supposed to. They're not your job! That's our job.

Your job is to write the movie, write the script, write the screenplay, produce, direct, and star! And then watch it. Just watch it! It's the Pat show. It's the Pat show . . . easiest production there ever was.

You just write it, write the screenplay, write the outline . . . this is what is going to happen, this is how it's going to work out, this is what I want to see . . . and then leave it to us. We'll fill in the blanks.

And then it dawned on me. What Anthony was telling me was to write something simple. It could be as simple as Pat wished for happiness and her wish was fulfilled. And then sit back, relax, and enjoy the movie as presented by my higher levels. If I tried to write it all, control it all, figure out how it was going to happen, put all the

IT'S YOUR MOVIE!

people and things in place, I would not get my wish. I would see a movie of Pat trying to run the show and control everything and I had seen that movie for too many years. I was tired of that movie. It was a movie of Pat looking for happiness. What I wanted was a movie of Pat finding happiness.

So now I am happily watching my movie. Scenes that would have caused me upset in the past are now just part of the movie. I don't re-act and re-create scenes I don't want to see. If what I see makes me feel bad and I am tempted to leave my theater and try and fix someone else's script or try and find someone to fix mine, I give my head a shake and know that there will be better scenes.

Since I am the only member of the audience in my theater, I don't have to please critics or worry about what others think of me. Other people can't even see my movie because they are in their own theaters watching their own movies. I might be playing a part in their movie, but if I stay in my own theater I can't see myself the way they see me. I can only see myself the way I see me. And I can only see them the way I write myself seeing them.

How I choose to see my movie creates my life. This is what Anthony means when he says, "Write the script the way you want to see it." My movie has a happy ending. I don't know how it ends and I don't know everything that happens in the movie. Sometimes I might want to close my eyes and skip over a part that makes me uncomfortable. I might even hold my breath for a minute, but it's *my movie* and I know it has a happy ending, so I am just going to take a deep breath, settle in, and watch with *joyful anticipation.*

CHAPTER 10:
YOUR MIND IS A PROJECTOR

I felt like such a failure. On the surface it appeared as though I had created a successful life. I was educated, owned businesses and homes, had friends and money in the bank. My children were well cared for and my husband loved me. But inside I felt like a failure.

It was fear again. I was desperate to learn how to use my mind to create the life of my dreams because if I could do that, I would never have to worry about it all being taken away and I could relax.

This was a project I had been working on for close to 30 years. I had read every book and tried every process I could get my hands on to learn how to control my thoughts and create the life of my dreams. My copy of Dr. Joseph Murphy's *Power of Your Subconscious Mind* was dog-eared, marked up, and highlighted. I had copied parts onto index cards and carried them with me for years. I affirmed with the best of them and practiced positive thinking until my cheeks hurt.

It seemed to be working for other people. Authors and coaches I have great respect for are still teaching similar techniques today. What was it about me? Why couldn't I get it? I knew that if I wrote a list of goals I could achieve most of them. But it was the ones I couldn't that stared me in the face. They were the ones I secretly didn't think I could achieve and they "proved" me right.

One of the first authors I ever studied, Napoleon Hill, said, "Whatever the mind can conceive and believe, it can achieve." So how was I going to make myself believe I could achieve what I wanted? Napoleon Hill also said, "The starting point of all achievement is desire." I had some experiences that caused me to believe that maybe the depth of my desire had more to do with it than how much I believed. So I moved from trying to talk my mind into believing I could achieve to trying to find things I wanted so badly the magnitude of desire would ensure their achievement.

Anthony's messages to me about who I really am and why I am here brought me comfort. I was no longer afraid of being judged and I no longer needed to seek outside approval. But . . . the part about the big ME running the show and transmitting the plan to my body for execution kind of stuck a bit. If that is the case, what should I do with the mind and emotional body I had created? Will I just float through life happily out of my mind?

I needn't have worried. Anthony heard my thoughts and was not about to leave me in that conundrum. There are three very strong themes that run through many of Anthony's messages. I say they are strong themes because Anthony had to work very hard to get the messages across to me, and because they held the keys that unlocked the door to my happiness and showed me how my mind and emotions played their roles. The themes are:

IT'S YOUR MOVIE!

1. It's your movie.

2. Your mind is a projector.

3. We create with our emotions not our thoughts.

We covered *It's Your Movie* in the last chapter and this chapter talks about how we create the movie of our dreams. These themes provided the keys I needed to find the happiness I had been searching for over 60 years to find. If they resonate with you, please know that I cannot do them justice in two chapters. Anthony's messages wound these keys in and around several others. He didn't just tell me some truths. He wove them together into a beautiful magic carpet. It took them all before I was ready to fly. I urge you to read the transcripts.

When Anthony first introduced the *It's Your Movie* theme I was excited and a bit surprised. His direction to *"write the script and let my higher levels provide the props and supporting actors"* seemed to make sense but it also made me a bit uncomfortable. It had tones of "think up what you want, ask for it, and we will provide it." This was something that had caused me serious discomfort in the past and seemed at odds with another theme: "Thoughts don't create—emotions create."

These themes appear and are woven through many of the transcripts. I chose three transcripts and excerpted bits from them to set the stage. In the twelfth session, Anthony talked about emotions and how we use them to create the movie of our life.

A: It's the emotions you transmit at the time you create that will determine what you will see on the screen. You are creating what you will see on the screen using the vibrational frequencies of the emotions you feel at the time you create. It's like a psychological test with children . . . "draw a picture." How they feel at the time gets painted onto the paper. Be very, very careful with emotional vibrational transmissions, for they are creating. They are "drawing" your life.

In the fourteenth session, Anthony talked about the difference between thoughts and emotions, and how one transforms and the other creates. He was explaining that it is not my thoughts that recreate or represent experiences that I don't want to see. It is my emotions.

A: Thoughts are things. They are waves. They go out and then they go around. They transform. It's like you taking the coal out of the ground and generating electricity, re-directing, harnessing, representing. It's like the revolving door. Emotions, now there's a different story. Emotions are blended particles of source energy. Emotions create experiences and experiences create emotions. Emotions therefore are blended source energy. It is source energy focusing source energy.

This message is somewhat circuitous. Anthony was having difficulty presenting a simple message because, as he said, *"There is not a framework, a physical plane framework to describe that, because the only types of creations for which there are frameworks and terminologies on the physical plane are the types that are redirecting. I take those materials, I make paint, I paint a picture, I have created a piece of art. I redirected the energy.*

In order to create emotions you must pull in energy from a source. It is also a redirection of energy, but it is a redirection of infinite source energy." Anthony went on to explain that emotion is a creative way to add energy to the physical plane. He said that not all emotions attract and use energy from the infinite source. Those emotions we label negative do not attract energy; those we label positive do. Positive emotions attract energy. Negative emotions dampen energy. This is a pretty big topic and I will leave it at that.

In the nineteenth session, Anthony talked to me about wants and desires and explained why I had not been entirely successful at creating the things I wanted in my life. Here is an excerpt from that channel:

A: Your mind is like a projector. The wants don't come from your mind. The wants come from our level. The wants come from our level through your mind and end up being projected on your screen of life . . . not by thinking, but by assessing and assigning feelings to the wants.

This idea took some time and several different types of "messages" before it started to become clear. The light came on one early morning as I lay in that semi-dream state where my brain was relaxed and the flighty waves of my fully conscious mind were quiet. I "felt" a want. "I want to be warm. I want to live in a place where my body is warm." This turned on the projector in my mind and I watched a series of images float across my inner screen. I was living in a place that looked and felt tropical. My house overlooked the ocean. It had a large covered lanai where I could work, entertain, or relax. The experience expanded. I was there and could feel it and hear it. It was morning and the air was warm. There was a bit of a breeze, the waves were breaking gently, seagulls squawked, and wet sand squished between my toes as I strolled down the beach. It was yummy!

Back to reality. It was late November and I was in my desert home where the morning temperatures were quite chilly, and by late afternoon it was too hot to sit in the sun. When the sun started to go down around five pm, it got chilly again. In my drowsy state I knew this wasn't what I wanted. I wanted a climate without the extremes where the temperature didn't get too hot or too cold and where I could be comfortable both inside and out.

As my brain waves speeded up and the images disappeared, I understood Anthony's message. *A: "Your mind is a projector, it is not a receiver or a transmitter."* The "want" message from ME to me was received while I was "out of my conscious mind" in a state similar to a meditative state. The message was actually received by my body, through the billions of little receivers on my body's cells.

My body received the message from ME and my mind was projecting the message as images that I could "see" and become emotionally connected with. This was how wants and desires came from what Anthony called *"our level."* I did not understand this before. I knew from experience that I could set goals and achieve them—as long as they were things I already knew how to do, like buying a new car when I had already bought a car or buying a new house when I had already bought a house.

I had also figured out that if I could get a really strong emotional attachment to something I had a better chance of creating a totally new experience. Trouble was, if I put something on my wish list that I had never achieved before, it was likely my emotional response would be fear, or unworthiness caused by disbelief, and there would be no way I could achieve the goal. As Anthony says, thoughts can re-create, but it takes emotions to create.

IT'S YOUR MOVIE!

In summary, what Anthony explained to me is wants or desires are sent by ME through the channel where they are received by my body. I feel these messages and they start the projector in my mind. The projector shows me different versions of how it could all work out. My emotional body assesses what it sees and creates emotional signals around what my mind is projecting. If my emotional body likes what it sees, it sends a signal that attracts source energy and my want is created. If my emotional body dislikes or is hesitant about what it sees, it sends out a corresponding signal. A hesitancy signal will usually result in my body giving my mind a "what about this?" scenario, and my mind projects the new scenario. This process can be played out over and over, and what gets projected as my life is a little of this and a little of that based on how my emotional body reacted to the movie my mind was projecting.

"So this is how it worked." Regardless of how hard I tried, how many programs I followed or books I read, I had not been able to use my conscious mind to create the life of my dreams. I had been able to make my conscious mind repeat experiences I had already created. When I wrote a list of things I would like to have in my life, I would somehow end up with those things UNLESS the things were related to acquiring or earning amounts of money that were far in excess of any amounts of money I had ever accumulated or earned, or they were things I had never before experienced, like unconditional love. I had written goals and made affirmations with the best of them, but try as I might, I could not make those goals come to pass.

My mind was practiced in analyzing, assessing, and judging. It made me good at many aspects of business. I was well compensated for critical thinking. My MBA thesis project was a feasibility study. It was how I rolled, and when Anthony tried to get across the need for me to stop doing that, to stop judging and assessing, I could accept what he was saying, but it was pretty much all I knew. I didn't know how else to be.

In our nineteenth channel, Anthony talked again about wants and desires and he could sense my confusion. I had tried very hard to use my mind to figure things out. I thought, researched, thought some more, tried some things I had learned, assessed the outcomes, and thought some more. Now Anthony was telling me to chill out and let my body talk. It sounded logical, but what would my mind do? What would I think about? Here is some of Anthony's advice.

A: Know who you are. Know that if you just let go, put it on autopilot, set it for joy, you will go where you want to, need to, should ... all of those words ... go.

So then how do you occupy your mind? What do you think about if you're not assessing or planning or judging? How do you occupy your mind? What is the point? That's what you think. "If my mind were to be totally free from anything ... I would be dead." That's what you think.

Your mind is like a projector. The wants don't come from your mind. The wants come from our level. The wants come from our level through your mind and end up being projected on your screen of life ... not by thinking, but by assessing and assigning feelings to the wants. "I want this ... well, is that a good thing? Is that really what I should do? How will it affect this? How will it affect that? I don't know how I feel about that." How you feel is uncertain. And what gets played on the screen is uncertain ... a little bit of this ... a little bit of that ... some good shots ... some bad shots ... not really certain.

IT'S YOUR MOVIE!

Change it around. Feel the wants. Feel the wants. They come in choices, bunches. (Here Anthony showed me a picture of bouquet of flowers.) *Pick the ones that feel good. Choose the wants that feel good and they will be displayed in beautiful living color on the screen of your life. Do not use your mind to search around for wants, to sift through them, to try and identify them, sort them out, assess them or grade them. NO. That only causes uncertainty, flickering, and bumps.*

Just let the wants come . . . like a smorgasbord of possibilities presented in a beautiful array. Choose the ones that feel good and let your mind project them. Let your mind project them. Do not worry how they will be acted out, how the scenes come together, who the supporting actors are, or where the props come from. Do not worry. Just choose the wants that feel good. Choose the wants that feel good. Do not assign grades or levels of want. Do not deal in "do not wants."

Practice. You will feel them . . . you will feel them. Pick the ones that feel the best. They are vague. They are not like words in your head or pictures. They're feelings. Become attuned to what feels good. Become attuned to your body. Sense it. Your body can give you the feedback at the time the want is sensed. Your body is receiving the options. Your body can discern. Do not use your mind for discernment. It cannot be used for discernment. The mind is not a receiver. The mind is not a transmitter. The mind is a projector. Let your body talk. Let your body talk. Let your body talk.

All these years I tried so desperately to get it. I kept my mind in overdrive, searching and trying to figure out what I really wanted, what would give me the life of my dreams. And the answer was so simple. Quit trying. Open up to the loving assistance that has been available from the beginning. Let my body be my partner. Let my body talk and listen to ME. Let it be. Just let it all be. Just BE. I had tied myself up in knots trying to figure it out and as I let my mind relax a whole new world opened up. I got enjoyment from the simplest things, a hummingbird, flowers, a child's laughter, or the wagging tail of a puppy dog. I let myself relax and gave my mind a much deserved rest. I felt a sense of freedom I had not previously known and something else, a lack of fear. My mind had been given the order to stand down and it was no longer on alert looking for danger. My body began to loosen up and it became easier to feel. In Anthony's words, I was learning to sit back, put my feet up on the back of the seat in front of me, and enjoy the show.

SECTION THREE

The Transcripts

CHAPTER 11:
ABOUT THE TRANSCRIPTS

When Anthony told me to use the actual transcripts of our formal channel sessions in the book, I balked. "Why would anyone want to read this stuff? It is mostly about me. People are interested in them, not me."

A: *Your reluctance to include these transcripts is all about you. It is not the real you. It is that ego again ... worrying and also wanting to do the best job possible for those who will read the book. We want to include the transcripts for them. Show them the value in having their own channel, their own frequency, their own two-way radio connection to higher levels. Show them what they might have heard through a third-party channel in a session devoted just to them. And then show them what it was like for you working directly with us. Give them an experience. Don't just ask them to jump in and see if they can swim.*

Maybe they won't read them all. It matters not. Offer them all.

Okay, I got it! Not only did I get my answer, I got another lesson on the value of opening your own channel. Anthony's message was accompanied by some little mind videos.

First I was shown a little boy being taught to ride a bike by an adult who said, "Okay, just sit on this seat and put one foot on a pedal. Now push off with the other foot and put it on the other pedal. Push on the pedals one foot at a time and you will be riding. One more thing before you go—try to look in the direction you want to steer. Oh, and don't lean too much one way or the other because you might fall over."

Next I was shown the same little boy being taught by a loving parent who explained how to do it, reinforced the parts the child didn't seem to understand, held the bike upright as the child began to pedal, made sure it was stable before letting it go, followed along closely, and grabbed hold again when the child started to wobble, all the while giving loving encouragement and praise.

In the next video, I was shown someone teaching a little girl to swim. "Okay, it might be a bit cold but just jump in and hold your nose. You should come to the surface and when you do, you will need to move your arms and legs to keep your head above water. Then lie on your back in the water and relax. You will float."

Then I was shown the same little girl learning from a loving parent. "Okay sweetheart, just jump in and I'll catch you. There, what a brave girl you are. Now lie back and I'll hold you up. Just relax. Good girl! Okay, now see what happens when I take one hand away. Good, you are floating. Good job! Now two hands. Wow, look at you! You can float all by yourself."

I was hesitant about including these little videos because they seemed a bit like likening us to little children who needed a mommy. Anthony was quick to point out that this was not the intent at all.

A: Fear is the biggest block to opening a channel. Fear is the only thing that can block love. Humans have been conditioned to fear. It was a requirement for safety in the early stages of the evolution of the human. It is deep-rooted and can only be overcome by love. Love is the one creative force. It is the source from which we all come. Your guidance realms are in another dimension, one that is untouched by fear. That is why we are the best source for guidance in your earthly journey. While you are on Earth, you cannot truly experience that level of love. The closest reference we can make is that of the love of a parent for a child. This is why we used these images.

Remember, you are not separate from us. You are not the weak being saved by the strong. We are all one. You are doing a magnificent job in the density of the physical environment. When you entered that realm, you lost the remembrance of who you really are and of your plan for this experience. We are here to help you remember. Word symbols cannot do the message justice. We are not here to provide guidance because you are weak. We are here to guide you back to the truth of who you really are and to help you remember. And, it is more than that because we can facilitate your plan. We can be of assistance. As I said, word symbols cannot do the message justice.

I got it—I just wasn't sure if I knew how to say it. So what I tried to do with these transcripts is paraphrase them at the beginning to show what an impersonal message would be like and then give you the whole shebang so you can get a feel for how it would be to have a guide there with you watching your reactions and gauging your readiness and level of understanding.

During the formal sessions, Anthony used my voice. I recorded the sessions and transcribed them later in the day, adding my comments and observations and any other information Anthony had given me through what I call our "silent channel."

I tried to use punctuation to give you a sense of what the recordings sounded like. The words Anthony spoke through me are in *italics*. My observations and silent communications are in regular font. I also attempted to round out the experience for you, to set the stage and the scene more fully by including notes and stories from my journal about what was happening in my life at the time and background about the visuals, physical sensations, references to dreams and other things that formed part of the formal channel session experience.

As you will see, it wasn't all an easy learning process. It didn't start rough and then just get better and better every day. Some days were good, easy and some not so much. My own headspace and physical energy level played a big part. At the same time, it was one of the most exciting things I had ever done, and I was hooked.

I can feel the energy of Anthony entering my body and sometimes the physical sensations are quite strong. This was especially true in the beginning. It was also somewhat like talking on a cell phone while driving down a remote mountain road. Sometimes the connection was strong and clear and sometimes it was weak and broken up. Channeling in the way I was doing it required a frequency match. Anthony needed to be able to transmit or communicate on a frequency that my body could accept and receive. Over time, I was better able to keep my mind from interfering with the frequency and I became more comfortable physically. This took practice and many admonitions from Anthony to *"relax"* and to *"keep your head out of the way!"*

Our first formal channel session happened on Feb 6, 2013. Between February 6 and March 31, I recorded 21 channel sessions. On March 31, Anthony's message and his tone changed. No more fooling around. I knew we were at the end of what was to be included in this book. I still channel; it has become a part of my life, my way of being. And, as a result of opening a channel, my life has changed in ways I cannot even begin to describe. All I can say is "Try it, you'll like it."

CHAPTER 12:
WEEK ONE

First Channel—February 6, 2013

This was the day of my first attempt at opening a channel. The experience of this first attempt is described in Section 1. I followed the process Sanaya Roman and Duane Packer outlined in their book, *Opening to Channel: How to Connect with Your Guide*. The total time on the recorder was 27 minutes and there were many physical sensations and gagging and groaning noises for the first half of the recording.

When Anthony finally began speaking in sentences, the voice was soft and clear and slow. As the words came out of my mouth, I was seeing them being printed on a big white screen in my mind. They were running from right to left and then turning and running from left to right and then right to left. They started from the bottom of the screen and worked up toward the top. It was like a ticker tape with the word appearing one letter at a time and I was saying the words as they appeared, almost like reading them.

Paraphrased message:

Based on my limited experience as a client of a psychic/intuitive, if I were to paraphrase this message as though I were the psychic/intuitive doing a session for someone, I would say something like this: "Your guide is saying something about a train and a lemon. Does that mean anything to you? He says his name is Anthony and he has been waiting for a long time and is very happy you have finally connected. He says you let something physical interfere with connecting with him before. He says he can take away your arthritis if you approve. He wants you to connect again. He says you have a lot do together and it will be fun."

Here is what Anthony said to me, through me, using my voice:

A: *A being of light and love, my name is fffff* ... (I remember thinking flower.) ... *Fffffffffala ... aaann ... ffaannn ...* (and then in a very clear and lower steady voice) *you are like a train, a steam engine, black ... it's lemony ... uhm hum ... mmm.mmm ... hmmm.mmmm.*

This type of noise continued for maybe a minute as the guide tried to master my voice.

And then the next part sounded almost like hacking something up.

A: *Call meeeeee Aaaaahhh ... ahhhh ... ahhh ... thony.*

And then things seemed to smooth out and the voice became steady and clear.

A: *I am Anthony, I have been waiting for you for many years. You are the one I chose. I am here to help you open your heart to love and joy and to help you shine this lighted message to the world. You have allowed some physical experiences to prevent us from meeting sooner. I am overcome with ecstatic joy and love for you and am supremely joyous that we are finally able to connect. I hope you will contact me regularly and that you will completely trust me for* **I am you and you are me and together we are we.** *I have waited here growing and learning so that I would be ready when you came.*

At this point the voice grew fainter and slower; the connection was thinning.

A: *We have much to do and we will have so much fun doing it. When you want to connect just float and I will catch you. Is there something you want to know now?*

I asked if he could take away the arthritis and joint pain in my hands and feet.

A: *Are you ready? Really ready? I can take it away anytime and you can approve. I will not take your power. I will assist if you approve. I will share it with you. We will be together . . . a team . . . a much stronger team.*

The voice had become very weak and then faded out.

Summary Notes:

In this first channel Anthony introduced the train visual. I could clearly see the train coming out of a mist. It was a black locomotive with steam billowing out of its stack and it was moving on a track towards me.

And, even as I write this some months later, I do not understand the relevance of Anthony's statement *"it's lemony."* My lips and mouth were being moved in a way that reminded me of sucking on something sour. Maybe this is what it was about.

I was pretty happy when I heard Anthony say he could take away my arthritis pain and I could approve. I thought he meant all I had to do was say something like "Go ahead, take it away, I approve." and "snap poofy" it would be done. As time went on and the subject came up again, I came to believe that when I asked Anthony if he could take away the arthritis and joint pain and he said, *"I can take it away anytime and you can approve,"* he meant that he could fix anything, but it was I who had created the pain and he could not fix it unless I approved at the level at which I had created it because I might just re-create it. This self-healing theme is one that would also continue and it is one that I still cannot quite understand.

As I listened to the recording of my first formal channel session with Anthony I was struck by two things. First, I found myself holding my breath, eager for the words to come out of my mouth, hungry for the next one. I had obviously been aware during the channel session and it was my voice I was hearing on the recorder and yet I had the feeling I was listening to someone else. This really gave new meaning to "I can hardly wait to hear what I'm going to say next."

Second, I was struck by the contrast between Sanaya and Duane's written accounts of their channeling with Orin and DaBen and what I was hearing on my recorder. Sanaya and Duane sounded so calm:

"We spent some time channeling Orin and DaBen and they asked us to . . . and explained how they wanted us to do it." My recordings were anything but smooth. The book had prepared me for physical sensations caused by different levels of energy and certainly did not promise perfection from the get go but I had visions of people channeling eloquently and easily and what I heard on my first recording was a lot of moaning and choking and gagging and words being almost regurgitated, with long pauses and wild variations in volume and tone. This was definitely not a nice neat voice like I had heard from the people channeling on YouTube.

And yet, I was thrilled. I had actually made a connection and channeled a higher level guide who used my voice. And I was very, very tired. The experience had taken a lot out of me and I felt drained, like a battery that had used up its energy and needed to be recharged. And, even though I had experienced it and listened to the recording, there was a part of me that couldn't quite believe I was channeling.

Second Channel—February 7, 2013

The very next morning, I wanted to try it again. It was still an awkward experience and the recording contains lots of gagging noises and deep breathing sounds, especially at the beginning before the speaking became clear. During that time, Anthony was silently telling me to open up, to relax and let it in.

The total time on the recorder is 27 minutes. The first words *"Dear One"* came after three minutes and then it took another minute of gagging and heavy breathing before the talking started again.

I had participated in a webcast group meditation that morning and was already in a relaxed meditative state, so it was easier to connect. I closed my eyes, relaxed, and floated through a door where I saw the council, and then Anthony began to speak using my voice.

Paraphrased message:

Your guide says he has a council for backup and support. He says you should give him your fears and he will transmute them on a higher plane. He says you are powerful and strong and cannot be harmed physically. He says that sore spot in your back comes from being afraid and resisting your own magnificence. He is telling you to put down your fears. They are like a bag of stones weighing on your shoulder. He says you are never alone and he has been with you helping you through this life. He says to get it clear what you want to talk to him about.

These are Anthony's words:

A: *Dear One . . . This is a fine day to talk. We have many things to talk about today. You are opening, opening like a flower . . . to me . . . and to my council. You met my council when you first came in the door. They are my backup, my support. They give me the help that I need to work with you in a way that you can handle.*

At this point I was experiencing jerking body movements. And Anthony was telling me to open up. He was trying to get me to relax so the energy would even out.

A: *We are going to become fast friends, you and I, as we go on this*

IT'S YOUR MOVIE!

journey of life experience. Open, Open, OPEN up to me. Open, open, I will take your fears and trepidations and help you to transmute them on the solar plane. All you need to do is give them up. Let them go! In many cases they are not even your fears, they are fears you have inherited or attached . . . or watched. They are fears of others, fears of you in other lives, fears of your mother, fears that do not serve you and you no longer need. You are strong, powerful, magnificent, and beyond, far beyond the reach of physical harm. You are you. You know who you are. You are one with the one. There is no need for you to be afraid of anything at all in this physical plane because there is nothing, Nothing, NOTHING at all that can hurt you in this physical plane.

Here the words are coming very slowly. The energy is waning and the connection is weak. Anthony then changes the tone and it becomes much more powerful. My physical energy is boosted and the channel clears again.

A: You are so, so, so POWERFUL. You are a GODDESS, you are creator, a QUEEN, a ruler. You are Cleopatra, my Cleopatra, and I promise to support you in this work on the physical plane because I know that it is not easy. I know that you have worked very hard and that you have felt alone many times. And I have watched and wanted . . . dreamed of being there to help you. And now, now I can because you have found me and asked me to come. And I will.

This next part is the beginning of Anthony helping me to remember what I came here to do. The channel is clear. He definitely has my attention.

A: There are so many things on this Earth that you can do . . . so many things. It matters not what you do. It matters only that you do it. That you, you, YOU do it. You have a job to do and your job is to help those on Earth to rewire, to open up, to expand, to lose their fears, to come into their own. You have been sent and it is now time for you to do your work. It is not a frightful job, it is just being you, the magnificent powerful you that you are. Just being you . . . coming out from under all of the things that held you down, all of the feelings, all of the terrors, all of the resistance . . . all of those things . . . you are just going to throw them off, throw them off. I'll catch them. I'll recycle them with the sun. You like to recycle, don't you? Well, that is what I'll do: I'll recycle them with the sun . . . and you, my lovely, will be free, free of all those things dripping and hanging and dragging, free to fly, free, free to be.

My mind started to wander and I began thinking about some of the things I wanted to do; this must have been interfering with the frequency of the channel, so Anthony was telling me to get my head out of the way. Then he changed the subject as he often does to get my "head out of the way."

A: Get your head out of the way. I can't see around your head. That spot in your back . . . you wanna know what that is about, that spot, that hurting, hurting spot? It's a resistance to magnificence. It's a fear . . . you are afraid to throw the sword . . . you are afraid of who will throw the sword . . . you're afraid of that spiked ball. Just watch it . . . just watch it.

And now Anthony introduced a visual to reinforce his message and keep my mind from wandering. He showed me a picture of a giant Hercules towering over me. And he was telling me that all the hardships and physical pain from past lives were done. The books Anthony refers to are the records of past lives stored in the Akash—something I learned later.

IT'S YOUR MOVIE!

A: There he is . . . Hercules. You've done these many, many times . . . with lots of hardships, physical pain and suffering. They mean nothing, NOTHING, they are gone. They mean NOTHING. It is all there written in the books, it means nothing . . . it's DONE, it's done.

Anthony then started to tell me about my job in this lifetime but the channel was growing faint and the voice was getting weaker. He was telling me to open up and breathe and then there were quite forceful gagging sounds on the recording as Anthony told me sternly to *"LET IT GO!"* I assume this was something coming up from the past to be let go.

A: Your job now is to be the light bulb . . . the filament . . . keep it coming . . . open up and breathe. There is something . . . and you are blocking it . . . Heeere it comes. (gagging and throwing up sounds) *Let it go, let it go, LET IT GO! . . . none of it means anything . . . let it all go, it is all over, it's all gone . . . let it go.* (gagging and heaving sounds again) *It's gone. It can have no more effect on you . . . let it go. Put down that bag of stones . . . it's pulling on your neck, it's pulling on your shoulder . . . it's heavy on your arm. PUT IT DOWN!*

That was quite a vigorous physical experience and Anthony quickly lightened up, changed the subject and introduced a calming visual.

A: Float . . . you see that lily pad, you see that little fairy. Float there . . . drink in the sun . . . you can do that any time you want. It's a rest.

I guess he thought I was over the worst, so Anthony started a different tone and subject. I was quite startled at first (and I was again startled when I listened to the recording afterward) because the voice here was quite loud and almost harsh sounding. This surprised me because to this point Anthony had felt very loving and soft.

A: QUIT WORRYING ABOUT MONEY. DO YOU KNOW HOW SILLY THAT IS REALLY?

Almost immediately the voice softened and I slowly realized that Anthony was not chastising me for worrying about money; he was imitating my self-talk and asking me to stop doing it.

A: *You can stop those. You can stop them. They do not serve you. They are not you. They are outside of you. They chastise and berate and belittle and nudge you into that fear zone again. Shift gears. Just shift gears. You don't need to be afraid of anything or anybody . . . you are me and I am you and together we are we. Let the resistance go. Let it go . . . hear me, feel me, see me . . . let it go. Take the sheet down . . . stand in your glory* (here the voice was emotional), *adore yourself . . . you can do it. I am going to help you, you are my friend and I am your friend.*

Up to this point in this session, I had not seen the teletype image of the words I was speaking like I did in the first session, but here I started seeing the teletype again. This is one of Anthony's ways of clearing the channel of my mental interference.

A: *And I see you can do it and I shall show you that it is so. We are a magnificent team and it's time we got started. Watch for it . . . watch for it . . . you don't even need to look . . . I'll just send it.*

At this point there was a smile in the voice.

A: *Don't worry at all about it. I'm just going to send it straight to you . . . it will just appear . . . and you do not need to even wonder who or when,*

IT'S YOUR MOVIE!

because I will look after the details. You need someone you can trust. You have been alone for a long, long time. You've not really been alone but you've felt alone. You were never alone but you did feel so very, very alone. I have had my arms around you many times for safety ... when your daughter was a baby ... and when she was a teenager ... many times ... and many times I watched as you suffered the pain of rejection and ridicule and could not understand why you felt you were being left alone. You grew ... like a beautiful tree you grew strong and willowy, able and free, and now we are together again, and I am here whenever you call on me.

Anthony is now telling me to start communicating with him, letting him be part of the team. The time for just tuning in and listening is over. I am to participate by asking him questions, not just about the big-deal things, but about the little things.

A: Get it clear, get it clear. Write it down, write it down. It doesn't have to be the be all and end all. Take it step by step. Join things ... do things ... ask me things ... anything ... little things ... big things ... anythings ... mmmhhmmm ... mmhhmmm ... next time, ask.

Summary Notes:

As I re-read this transcript, it is clear to me that we were both feeling our way. Anthony was learning how to talk to me and I was learning how to open up and allow it. He knew everything that was happening in my life—all my feelings and emotions and was trying to work with it all.

"*Get it clear*" is another of those phrases that will continue to pop up. It seemed that every time I thought I had found something I wanted I would roll it around in my mind and assess it until I found something "not quite right" with it and then I would start to look for something better. And so it went, round and round, trying to use my conscious mind to create instead of just following the feelings and desires. I would tell myself, "Get it clear what you want" and then think, "But if you get it clear that is what you will get and there could be something better and what if it only works so many times before you've had your turn"— mind games.

The beauty of establishing your own connection with your higher levels is that they know these things about you, and they can help you unravel the games.

Third Channel—February 8, 2013

This day, while reading the channeling book, I started a silent communication with Duane Packer's guide DaBen. For some time I had noticed tightness in various areas and muscles of my body. I often felt as though my body was braced for a blow or preparing to run. That day I was feeling the tension and tightness in my right thigh. I would consciously relax it and in no time it would be tight again. In silent communication, I asked DaBen for help in changing this and in releasing the tension. DaBen responded with a question. "Do you really want it changed? Your body will change."

"I'm not sure, what will it look like?"

DaBen responded, "It will be different . . . softer . . . different."

IT'S YOUR MOVIE!

My response was quick and came from years of worrying about my body image. "Not fat, not fat, not fat." I really wanted it changed and I really wanted to control the outcome or to at least preview it before I made a decision—a familiar refrain.

I then started the recorder and prepared to do a formal channel session with Anthony. It took almost six minutes during which time I was making gagging sounds and floating and searching for a connection before Anthony started speaking. The total elapsed time on the recorder was 25 minutes.

Paraphrased message:

Perhaps a more talented intuitive than I could see through this communication and come up with some useful words for me. Without the background and maybe without the visuals and certainly without the emotions, I would find most of this a confusing jumble of words. Maybe I would offer something like this: "Your guides say you have some old fears and they have taken them away. They also say you are too wrapped up in physical appearance and you should let go of that. They say you have a fear of expansion because you think there is some limit and there is not. They say you are ready to fly forward, to expand, and they will help. They say you should keep moving, following your instincts. They say your mind likes to be in control and they would like you to set that aside and develop new skills like channeling and hypnosis. They say you are funny and that works for you."

Here are the channeled words:

A: We're releasing it, you see. It's going to take a while ... there's a lot of dead stuff in there ... a lot of dead ... many, many dead. We can work on it with you, and we will. We're both here, you know ... Anthony and DaBen.

This was something Sanaya and Duane said could happen—that we could call on other guides as well as our own.

A: We're kicking it into high gear. It's going to be happening fast now ... let it go, let go, LET IT GO.

Here they were showing me a visual of a person walking a tightrope in a big circus arena. The person had a long pole for balance and was carefully walking along the wire high above the crowd. When they get to the part about *"you have wings"* there is laughter in the voice.

A: It's a high wire act. It's a tightrope. You've been walking it afraid, afraid that you might fall and yet exhilarated by the walk. There's a net, you know. But you don't need to do that ... you have wings. Just fly to the other side. Climb down the ladder and wave goodbye to the crowd. You're finished with that act. It's all over ... the tension ... the fear ... the tightrope ... it's gone ... peww.

I'm not sure how to write that sound (peww); it sounded something like an elastic band twanging and then the image was gone. Next, Anthony produced a video of the train and then a heart-shaped door. It opened and butterflies flew out.

A: And now, now we see ... oh, it's your locomotive. That's not what we want you to see. You need to be ready for it ... open to it. Open the door ... open your heart ... see the butterflies coming out ... so pretty.

IT'S YOUR MOVIE!

As often happens when new visuals are introduced, the subject was changed.

A: You're too wrapped up in the physical . . . the body thing. It's part of the female. It's part of the hard route you chose. You've done a great job, magnificent. Now it's time . . . it's time to ditch all that . . . all those emotions that don't serve—sub-optimal, the fears, the lack of self-worth, the trust issues . . . time to let them all go now. It's time. It is time. IT IS TIME TO MOVE FORWARD. YOU COULD FLY IF YOU WANTED TO. BUT NOT YET WHERE YOU ARE, NOT YET.

Now I am being shown walls that are closing in on me and Anthony is asking me to stay present in the physical plane. I had been feeling spacey and sometimes wondering why I couldn't just float off into another dimension and leave the world and its problems behind.

A: Stay in that plane. It feels like it's closing in on you but it isn't. It's helping you. You can't see that. It's making you stronger . . . in that realm. Stay in that realm. You'd like to float out, past, through, around. Press play. Take it off hold and press play . . . open up, open up, OPEN UP. You're like a flower . . . only when you fully blossom, you will transform the world. You will become something you never imagined . . . nobody has ever imagined. You have that fear. Let it go, let it go, LET IT GO . . . that fear that if you blossom that will be it, that there's some limit to how you can expand. That something is limiting, that there is some limit.

For some time I had held a niggling fear that if I really let it all go, opened up to the world of possibilities, quit worrying about what others thought of me and how I was doing in the neighbor's eyes, I would be utterly, completely, and totally alone. I think Anthony was trying to reassure me here that there was no limit to how much I could let go and expand and that if I could really do it, the result would be so wonderful I couldn't even imagine it.

A: There is no limit. There is no limit. You can't imagine it, you can't imagine it, just keep going, just keep going, and as you see it, as you see the new, you will see the NEW and then you will be able to imagine more but you can't see it from here. You can't SEE there from here, just keep going, don't worry about what it looks like in the end, you can't know from where you are, you can't know, just GO, JUST GO. Don't worry about your luggage.

This is a reference to an unsettling and recurring dream I was having. I was in a rush to go somewhere and didn't have time to pack my luggage or couldn't find the airport or didn't have a ticket.

A: Or if you've got everything sorted out to make it right on the other end. You don't know what the other end looks like, you don't know what you need, JUST GO, we'll provide it, we'll make sure it's there. In fact it's hard for us to provide it when you settle in to worrying about what you need to take because then you close us down, you take over, you put the line on hold. Take the hold button off, throw it away, we don't need hold, just go, JUST GO. It doesn't matter. It doesn't matter. You're prepared. You're ready. YOU ARE READY AND WE WANT TO HELP YOU GO, to fly forward, to expand. It doesn't need to be hard and there is no limit. There's no limit. It's not confined to pages or screens or things you can see in your mind. THERE IS NO LIMIT, THERE'S NO BOX. IT'S BEYOND YOUR KEN... WITH YOUR EARTH MIND... IT'S BEYOND YOUR KEN. IT WILL BE SHOWN IN STEPS... STAGES. GO TO THE NEXT ONE AND THEN YOU'LL SEE FARTHER. IT'S LIKE A DARK ALLEY.

IT'S YOUR MOVIE!

Here Anthony was showing me a visual of me walking in a dark alley. I could see only a small distance ahead and as I walked forward I could see a little further down the alley.

A: IT'S NOT REALLY . . . you know, you just can't see it, you can't see ahead that far. As you get nearer you can see it. Don't worry about it. Don't worry about seeing it. YOU WILL FIND IT. And we can guarantee you that it will be wonderful and you won't be disappointed in what you find. Just go, keep moving. Keep moving. KEEP MOVING. If it hurts, we'll help. You don't really need our help, because it only hurts because you can't see, it only hurts because you become afraid because you can't see what it'll look like but you DON'T NEED TO SEE WHAT IT WILL LOOK LIKE. WE CAN GUARANTEE YOU, YOU WILL LOVE IT! YOU WILL LOVE IT!

I attended lots of training events and seminars over my business career and a team building exercise facilitators seemed to love was one where you built trust by falling backwards knowing that your team would catch you before you hit the ground. At least that was how the exercise was designed and how I always saw it work. Although, I must admit that I wondered on occasion what would happen if I just stepped back and let someone fall.

A: It's like those games they play in seminars, where somebody falls backwards and people catch them. Well, we're the catchers . . . (here there is laughter) *only we don't want you to go backward, we want you to keep moving—like the train.*

The topic has come around to include the physical again, reminding me to quit worrying about the physical. Anthony then moves on to reminding me to keep my controlling mind out of it.

A: JUST KEEP MOVING. Get up a head of steam and MOVE. It doesn't mean physically move, moving your body, or worrying about what's your body going to look like if you don't do this or you eat that, or you drink that, or you do this—that's not what we mean. We mean KEEP MOVING, KEEP DOING. FOLLOW YOUR INSTINCTS. YOUR INSTINCTS ARE VERY, VERY GOOD. YOU HAVE THE HIGHEST TRAINING, SO HOW COULD YOUR INSTINCTS BE ANYTHING BUT THE HIGHEST . . . YOU ARE A TREMENDOUS BEING. We want you to see what you are talking about, so we are going to provide you with an experience so that you will have NO DOUBT AT ALL! We're going to give that to you because you deserve it. Not only because you deserve it but because YOU ARE IT.

We know how your Earth mind works, that it likes to be in charge, that it likes to design and control and judge and do all those things. We know how that works. You've used those skills very well in this lifetime and in many other lifetimes. We know you are good at that. Those skills are not the ones we want you to continue to hone. Set them aside, just set them aside and develop your new skills, your channeling, your hypnosis, your ability to relate to the birds and the animals and the people. Develop those skills (here in a happy, laughing voice) *and we are going to give you a party.*

We are going to give you something so fantastic that you are gonna wanna do it. YOU ARE GOING TO LOVE IT! YOU ARE GOING TO JUST LOVE IT! CHICK A BOOM, CHICK A BOOM, YOU'LL JUST LOVE IT! You're funny, don't lose the funny, you're good at it, it works, it draws people in, it attracts them. Keep the funny, keep the funny . . . AMEN.

IT'S YOUR MOVIE!

Summary Notes:

This was a longer, wandering message that might have been summed up in a few simple statements. Ditch the fear. Keep moving, keep doing things. Follow your instincts. But they would have gone in one ear and out the other. Without the full experience, the visuals, the references to other things going on in my life, the humor and the repetition, I would not have received and perhaps most importantly would not have internalized the full message.

I sincerely hope you learn to do this for yourself. I have not found anything as comforting or as welcome as the experience of being talked to by an entity or entities that have only my best interests, my happiness, and my success in mind. I am grateful for the length of the messages, for it is not just the content that is so important—it is the conversation, the experience.

Fourth Channel—February 9, 2013

This is the fourth formal channel session. I started the recorder when I sat down to open the channel. The total time on the recorder is 29 minutes. Speaking started after seven minutes. There were some heavy breathing and groaning sounds before the actual speaking started. As with every day so far, my mouth was being moved, my lips pursing and being sucked into my mouth as Anthony opened up the channel and prepared my body for him to speak through.

I was still searching and testing out ways to get the channel open. This day I started by reading out loud and recording the first part of the relaxation exercise in the *Opening to Channel* book. My plan was to record myself reading the exercise and then listen to the recording each time I sat down to open the channel with Anthony. The exercise starts out with deep breathing, and before I could get to the part I wanted to read and record, Duane's guide DaBen appeared in my head and I could feel Anthony starting to prepare the channel.

I was not yet comfortable with Anthony's message that I was to write a book about our channeling experience. "Maybe it wasn't really Anthony, maybe I misunderstood." My mind was also whirling with details. "I think I see 14 chapters . . . does it have 14 chapters?" I was confused and uneasy, so before I went to bed the night before, I called on Anthony and said, "I have some questions I would like you to answer in our next channel session. Am I supposed to transcribe these channeled messages and write a book? Does it have 14 chapters? Will you help me?"

Paraphrased message:

"Your guide is telling you to get on with writing the book. He also wants you to stop worrying about details and try to keep your mind out of the way when he is talking to you. He is telling you that a channel is like an instrument or pen and that if you just sit down at your computer and start to type it will come. He says you are magnificent and that you should get your questions clear for the next session."

How Anthony says it:

A: Here we are again . . . . we come again . . . .

IT'S YOUR MOVIE!

. . . . ouuuhhhh . . . . mmmmmm . . . . (Here there are gagging noises but they are less vigorous than the days before.) *. . . . .* (Here there is heavy breathing and soft moaning sounds.) *. . . mmmmmmmmm . . . mmmmmm* (I can feel Anthony opening up the voice box.) *. . . hmmmhmmm . . . YOU . . . are punctual, right on time. It's all good . . . mmhmm . . . today . . . Today . . . todayyyyyy isss a . . . nother . . . d . . . ay . . . a . . . nd the first week of writing the book.* (Now the channel is working well and the voice is smooth and even.) *It's what we want you know. We, we REALLY want you to do this and we're here to help you.*

So I had my answer. Yes, they really want me to write a book.

A: You need to get your head out of the way. Get your head out of the way, we can't see. You worry so much. Is it right? Do it now. Get it done! We're going to rewire you so you don't do that so much . . . going to help you do that. Mmm (Here Anthony was laughing.) *like a kitten, playing, playing with a string.*

Anthony began showing me little videos to help make his points. The first was a kitten sitting on the floor swatting at a string that was being dangled in front of it. And then came a book floating in the air.

A: You'll be free, free of all those worries, just playing with it, having fun, in the light, playing. It's there you know. It's all there. It's been there for a long time just waiting for you. You can see it can't you? Yes, you can. It's all done, it's all printed, beautiful, floating there for you, just reach out and take it, open it up, feel the pages, look in wonder.

Anthony was laughing again, trying to help me see how much fun writing this book will be and how happy I will be when it's finished. I could see myself looking at the book floating in front of me. I had a big smile on my face as I reached out and took the book in my hands.

A: You did it! You did it! And they love it! Of course they do, of course they do. They're attracted to it. It's for them. It's for them. Through you for them. Oh, you are excited, you are so happy. Yes, it's a beautiful day ... mmhmm ... Don't put it back, don't put it back, hold it! Feel it! Yes, it's yours.

I could feel my mind starting to push in with doubts and questions and I had the urge to put the book back.

A: It's yours ... who's going to publish it? Don't worry. Don't worry about that. Let us do that please. Let us help.

Anthony was laughing again as he gently chided me for worrying.

A: You are already deciding, worrying about this and that and how many chapters and on and on. You'll know ... YOU'LL KNOW ... you'll see it.

At this point Anthony changes the theme and begins to tell me what a channel is and what it means to channel.

A: You want to channel ... you know what that means? You're the instrument. You're the INSTRUMENT ... YOU ARE THE PEN. Sit down at your computer and type ... it'll come.

And now I get a little ego lesson. The wonderful thing about Anthony is he can read my mind. He knows every thought that passes through.

IT'S YOUR MOVIE!

I don't really need to talk to Anthony out loud or even silently. He hears my thoughts. We are accustomed to having our thoughts be private. That Anthony could read my mind was something that took some getting used to. Here he could tell that part of me was warming to this writing a book idea because maybe I would get some attention and notoriety out of it.

A: You really want to be involved, to take credit. That's not really you. That's that ego thing sitting on your shoulder. Give it a wink, give it a nod... tell it to BRUSH OFF... We've got work to do here.

Once I got over the embarrassment of having my mind read and having it come out in a recorded session that would be in the book, I was interested in Anthony's "Tell it to BRUSH OFF." This is not wording that I would have used. I might have used something a bit more vulgar. In fact when I was listening to the recording and typing the transcription for the book, the little voice in my head said "Tell it to BUGGER OFF!" and I had to rewind a bit to hear what was actually said.

A: See that beautiful shaft of light pouring through the window, the one that was shining on the kitten? And now it's coming through shining on an empty space on the kitchen floor.

Now we were back to the subject of channeling and Anthony was showing me a little video.

A: STEP INTO IT. Feel it pouring over you. Feel the warmth, the love, the light. That's all it is. THAT'S ALL IT IS. Just open up, move to where the light is. Let it shine on you and pour right through. That is what a channel is.

Here Anthony laughed as though to say, "How easy is that?" or perhaps, "Get over yourself."

A: That's how you do it! Is it too easy for you, too simple? Doesn't need an MBA. Oh well, oh well, OH WELL. There isn't a right time or a wrong time. There isn't a right computer or a wrong computer.

Reading my mind again—I had been wandering into "procrastination by details'—thinking that my old computer probably wasn't up to the job and I had better stop this book stuff for a bit and research a new computer.

A: There's only opening up and letting it POUR RIGHT THROUGH. Just let it pour right through. You don't need to wait for the recognition that comes from a successful book and a speaking career.

Here Anthony begins again to tell me how magnificent I am and that we are a team. He is also reinforcing that the book is already written and waiting in another dimension. Our job is to get it into this plane and into your hands.

A: You're already magnificent. You cannot be more magnificent. YOU CANNOT BE MORE MAGNIFICENT! YOU CANNOT BE MORE LOVED! YOU CANNOT BE MORE RECOGNIZED! YOU are YOU and I AM YOU AND TOGETHER WE ARE WE. THIS BOOK IS OURS.

Anthony uses a lot of voice tones and inflections to help get the point across. The words in capital letters were all being said slowly and with emphasis.

IT'S YOUR MOVIE!

A: Did you hear that? OURS . . . WE WILL DO IT! I CAN'T DO IT WITHOUT YOU AND YOU CAN'T DO IT WITHOUT ME . . . BECAUSE IT'S ALREADY HERE, HERE WHERE I AM . . . AND YOU ARE ALREADY THERE . . . THERE WHERE THEY ARE . . . and that's how it works. THAT'S SIMPLY HOW IT WORKS. Your part is to make it physical. Make it so that THEY can see it.

Anthony is once again having a bit of fun and laughing. If you were in my living room listening to the channel session going on or to the recording playing afterward as I typed, you could hear the message. But you aren't, so it is up to me to try and get the message across with words.

*A: They can't see me, but through you they can hear me. But there aren't many of them sitting in your living room, are there? So, we need to get to them, and the easiest way to do that is to write in a book . . . an Earth book. Write it down . . . print it on those beautiful pages . . . see the printing . . . see those **beautiful** pages and that lovely blue cover . . . isn't it nice?*

Here Anthony was showing me a little video of the book, turning the pages and then showing me the cover.

A: They'll like it, too. YES, and then, they'll want to hear more about it . . . there'll be more . . . this is just the tip of the iceberg . . . the beginning . . . the bud . . . see it?

And now a video of a little rose bud in a garden. It was slowly opening up to bloom and then there was a little bee buzzing around the plants and flowers.

A: You see it? It's like one little bee going out to the plants and gathering that luscious pollen, luscious, healthy, feeding pollen . . . flies back to the hive and shares it . . . and there are so many of them doing that. You're all a wonderful, wonderful bunch of gatherers and feeders . . . busy bees . . . busy bees. Often flying way farther than you need to, to get to the best flowers.

Anthony was chuckling, having a bit of a laugh at us for "flying farther than we need to get to the best flowers." I think he was saying, "If you would just let us help, it would be so much easier."

A: But I've already told you enough about that . . . so let's get on with it. Here we go. Here we go . . . there's your train. Chugga chugga chugga chugga, chugga chugga . . . here we go, the conductor is ringing the bell . . . ALL ABOARD. There you are, sitting in your seat, the sun shining in the window . . . the light . . . writing . . . writing in your pad . . . smiling. You're on your way. You're on your way . . . to heaven.

The train video is one of Anthony's favorites. This time he was showing me inside the train, happy to be writing and being on my way. The last word "heaven" was said very softly, almost like he was hesitant to say it.

A: Nnnnoooo, I can't give it to you all at once. That's not how it works. I CAN'T, IT'S TOO MUCH. Just take it BIT by BIT . . . write it, organize it, keep your little mind busy making it pretty . . . and DO NOT WORRY! THERE IS BUT ONE MESSAGE AND THAT MESSAGE IS LOVE! Feel it! Wrap it in a story! Tell them! TELL THEM. They want to hear. They need to hear. They need to know that they are safe and loved as well . . . that they are MAGNIFICENT . . . that GOD LOVES THEM. They need to know that . . . and that's the game.

IT'S YOUR MOVIE!

Anthony was reading my mind again. I was thinking, *Can't we just sit down and write this and get it over with?* And then he was laughing and joking, trying to lighten it up and soothe my mind to keep it out of the way.

A: *Pretty high-stakes game ... In for a penny, in for a pound. You might not like all of this ... in your physical Earth mind. YOU MIGHT NOT ... but you'll love it just the same.*

I was starting to get frustrated with the wandering message and lack of specifics. If I had to write a book, I wanted details, dammit! The channel was dimming and the words were becoming very quiet and draggy.

A: *I'm going to need to go now ... Yoouu ... seem ... to ... be ... getting ffrustrated ... with ... the ... lack ... of ... concrete ... details ... in these ... sessions. What we did today was answer the question you put forward last night. You wanted to know if this was really what you were meant to do ... if it ... if you were really meant ... to write ... this book. That ... was ... your question ... as I understood it ... And today I ... gave ... you ... the ... answer. Remember ... sweetness ... you need to get it clear, GET IT CLEAR ... when you have a question, get it clear ... know that your question will be right ... it will be in the highest ... it will come from above ... from you ... and will be PERFECT. Settle in, feel it, feel the question.*

I think what Anthony was referring to in that section was my tendency to be indecisive. "Is this question the best I can ask? Is this really what I want to know? Will this get the best answer?" Anthony was urging me to trust myself to listen to the inner voice of the higher me and the question will be clear and perfect. He was also asking me to trust my intuition. And then, the channel cleared somewhat as Anthony put more energy into the final bit.

A: Okay, here . . . you like to have structure, so this is how we'll do it. We'll do it this way. Every day, feel it, get the question, FEEL IT, FEEL IT, and then, before you go to sleep at night or in the evening, WRITE IT DOWN. Write it down and then we'll know, we'll both know, and then when we connect, you'll have your answer. And know that I'm always there . . . just RIGHT THERE . . . and will be giving you nudges and help and hugs, so when you hear those little things, know them to be me. KNOW THEM TO BE ME . . . and now . . . ADIEU.

Summary Notes

The ending of this session may seem rather abrupt, but it is only the spoken session that ends that way. Anthony is signaling the end of what I am to record and transcribe, but Anthony does not leave that quickly. The channeling state is one of such love that it would be hard to break the connection that quickly. It is similar to loved ones lingering over a goodbye at an airport or train station, so our sessions continue with Anthony speaking directly to me.

Fifth Channel—February 10, 2013

This is the fifth formal channel session and the total time on the recorder is 31 minutes. Anthony started speaking at four minutes. Until that time, I was doing breathing exercises and Anthony was preparing the channel. As with the first four times, my eyes were rolled upward, my eyelids were drawn down tightly, my mouth watered, my lips moved as though warming up and my throat was cleared. For the first four sessions, I experienced gagging and heaving, but today it was only coughing and throat clearing. And today, as with all four previous sessions, my eyes watered during the session in the same way they would if I saw or experienced something of great beauty that "brought tears to my eyes." When the session ended, my cheeks were wet.

It was getting easier to open the channel and I was becoming more confident that Anthony would show up and talk.

Yesterday during our channeling session, Anthony asked me to get it clear, to write down my question for the next day's channeling. He asked me to write it down at night before I went to sleep. So last night it crossed my mind several times, and I thought, *later*. Finally, just before I was going to drop off, I got a pen and paper and wrote down the question. This was the question as I wrote it: "Is it in the highest interest for all concerned for me to continue to learn and practice Quantum Healing Hypnosis Therapy (QHHT)?" During the night I dreamt about this question.

The paper on which I had sleepily written my question about QHHT had some earlier writing on the flip side. They were also questions. They were questions I had written during my QHHT training and I planned to use them in meditation. One of the questions was "Why did I create arthritis in my hands and neck, hips and legs, ankles, feet and wrists?"

I had been awakened in the night by severe pain on the right side of my back, neck, arm, elbow, wrist, and hand. It was bad enough that I considered getting up to take some pain killers, but decided against it and was eventually able to get back to sleep. The pain was still there when I woke up this morning and I was again considering pain killers. Before getting out of bed, I had a silent conversation with Anthony.

Anthony explained that I am made of light, a light being, and I create pain in my physical body by blocking energy at certain points. He also explained that since I am light, my body should not feel cold (I had been feeling chilled). Anthony worked with me to visualize a dial like a thermostat inserted in my body at areas where I felt pain. I could see those areas as frozen, cold, and tight. As I dialed up the "energy thermostat" that part of my body would relax and the pain would gradually lessen. We kept doing this, moving the thermostat around to the blocked areas until I felt warmer and the pain had virtually disappeared.

Anthony referred to both the dream and our silent conversation this morning in the formal channeling session.

Paraphrased message:

"Your guides and your higher self are always with you. You want to help people and you can. You doubt it but you can do it. You can do both QHHT and channeling. They will both work. Whatever you want to do is valid. Just go for it. Your life is like a movie. It's your movie and you can create it the way you want it. Love yourself enough to create your own happiness. Abundance is the natural state. Do not worry about abundance."

IT'S YOUR MOVIE!

Anthony's words:

A: Aahhhhhh . . . aahhhh . . . umhmmm . . . see the point of light? Umhumm . . . open up to it . . . OOhhhhawwww . . . (sounds of throat clearing.) . . . umhmmmm . . . uhhuh . . .

Anthony is coming through now and he starts with the train visual. The train is coming toward me and Anthony is singing and chuckling. As has happened before, when Anthony speaks the word *heaven* it is done with a soft, almost reverent voice.

A: I see that train a comin', comin' down the track. I ain't seen heaven, since I don't know when. Good morning. We're finally here. It took a bit today. Needed to get you laughing to get you loosened up. We saw you this morning . . . amping it up, visualizing, getting rid of your own pain. You're gettin' it. You're getting it. You're so powerful, so, so powerful.

Here Anthony is showing me a little video of a bird sitting on a branch singing its heart out. He is also still trying to lighten me up with the chick-a-boom thing and a chuckle.

A: Just loosen up, loosen up and let flow. Oh, just love it . . . chick-a-boom. See that little birdie, no worries, just singing a song, singing a song. You think he's worried about the weather? Nooo. He's singing a song, singing a song. Rolling along, singing a song. Loosen up . . . loosen up.

Now Anthony is introducing what will become a recurring theme—"It's your movie!" He is showing me a big movie screen and then me in a director's chair.

A: See the big screen. See the big, big white screen. Yeah, it's waiting for you. It's waiting for you to create the next scene. That's all it is you know, it's just a screen and a scene and you are the creator, the director, and the producer. Just put in your order, tell us what you need, we'll provide the actors and the materials and the STUFF. Just create it. What is it you want to see on that big white screen? What is it you want to see? Create it!

As he often does when my attention starts to wander and thoughts begin to creep in, Anthony switches topics and introduces a different video. My mind had veered off into Worryland and Anthony picked up on it. First he is showing me the bird sitting on a branch again and then the bird flies around.

A: See that little birdie? He's not waiting for it to happen. He doesn't want confirmation before he moves forward . . . no he sits there, he sings, he flits, he flies. He's just doing it. No waiting . . . no needing . . . just living . . . living large. Flying, he's flying, singing, and flying. What goes in comes out. He doesn't hold anything, doesn't wait for anything. He's just being . . . just being. You can do that too . . . and you can help other people.

Anthony is now using one of my favorite things— helping other people— as a teaser to get me to listen. And he brings up my experience in the night and this morning with the pain in my body and him helping me visualize turning up the energy dials to ease the pain. Anthony can also sense that I am still not convinced that I am able to help people heal.

A: That's really what you want to do, isn't it? . . . help other people. You know we created that pain in you last night so you could experience it and you could experience getting rid of it yourself . . . so you could

IT'S YOUR MOVIE!

KNOW *you could do that for other people. You know that! And yet you still doubt it. You know it. You saw it, you experienced it, and you doubt it.*

Here Anthony is telling me that they will help me get over the doubt. And as time went on, they did. Next Anthony is talking about the dream I had last night with the two hearts representing QHHT and Channeling. The voice was quite strong where I used capital letters.

A: *We'll take that doubt away. We can do that. We'll make it easier for you. We'll help. You had a question, you wrote it down. And, we have an answer. You saw part of it in your dream, the dream with the hearts . . . AND HERE'S THE REST. DO IT! GO FOR IT! DO THEM BOTH! THE MORE WAYS YOU CAN HELP YOUR BEAUTIFUL BROTHERS AND SISTERS THE BIGGER IT WILL GROW, THE BIGGER YOU WILL GROW, AND AS YOU GROW, IT GROWS . . . LIKE A BIG BEAUTIFUL BALL OF GLORIOUS BLUE LIGHT. GO FOR IT! EXPAND! MOVE FORWARD! YOU CAN DO ANYTHING YOU WANT! ANYTHING! JUST GO! DO IT! WE'RE HERE. WE'LL HELP . . . although you don't really need that help.*

Anthony is now reinforcing that I can do it and they are always with me and want me to connect. He means this for everyone, not just me.

A: *You can do it! You have all the tools! You know what to do! CONNECT! CONNECT! The better part of you . . . not better in a judgment way, but the bigger part of you is here with us. YOU have so much power, so much ability. THERE IS ABSOLUTELY NO REASON TO DOUBT! GO FOR IT!*

For some time I had been waking in the early morning hours with vague memories of night dreams and then drifting back into a deep sleep with quite vivid dreams. I remembered these vivid dreams when I awoke and they seemed more like current visions of my life as I would like it to be. The dreams in the night were more like those "huh?" dreams we have. Again Anthony is having fun when he gets on a word roll and is chuckling.

A: Those dreams you see, the ones in the morning when you think you are just drifting, visualizing, no . . . you can have those. That can be! Go for it! Create it! LOVE IT! HAVE FUN! SING! DANCE! FLY! FLIT! (chuckle) *YOU are creator incarnate!*

Here Anthony is introducing a new visual to support his message that I am creating my life. He was showing me a big long quill pen with a beautiful picture flowing out of the nib.

A: Your physical being is like the quill on a big long pen. Most of it, including the ink well, is on this side. All you need to do is move the nib. Draw the picture . . . write the scene. It'll flow to you. It'll flow to you just like the ink flows to a pen . . . beautiful! beautiful! . . . magic pen . . . any colors you want, any size. You're the driver, the painter, the operator. Make it what you want. Don't settle. Love yourself. Love your beautiful, magnificent, creative self. LOVE YOURSELF ENOUGH to create HAPPINESS!

Another new visual— this time a little girl standing looking up at a bright star.

A: You see that star and that little girl? That's what she wanted, that's all you want . . . happiness. Happiness for you and happiness for everyone. Do your part. Create the scenes . . . ask for help.

IT'S YOUR MOVIE!

I had read somewhere that when you find feathers or pennies or whatever you identify as a sign, it is a reminder that your guides and angels are with you, watching you, supporting you and loving you. Anthony reinforced that idea with words and pictures of moonbeams, sunshine, feathers, and pennies.

A: We're right here. I'm right here, always and forever . . . Loving you, shining you. See the moonbeams, you know it's me. See the sunshine, know I'm there. See the feathers and the pennies . . . love notes.

Here Anthony is again sensing that I am tempted to visit Worryland and is asking me to open up and not wait for outside validation and to accept myself the way I am.

A: I would really like you to open up, to relax, to soar, and to go with it. To not wait for validation. You are valid! Whatever you do, whatever you want is valid. Valid for all eternity. You don't need any more validation. I would like for you to accept your physicality the way it is. Accept your talents and gifts. Accept our love. You don't need to prove. You've already anted up. You're paid up!

The visual presentation in this part of the message was of a counter at a butcher shop with one of those little machines that dispenses slips of paper with numbers on them to help people wait their turn. He showed me standing in front of the little machine pulling one numbered slip after the other and keeping them all. And he showed other people lined up in front of other butchers and little machines.

A: By receiving you are not taking. You are accepting. And, there's a big, big difference. Accepting is an act of love. Taking is a withdrawal. I would like you to stop withdrawing and start accepting.

I've got so much lined up there for you (chuckle) *waiting for you to accept it. Just take one, just like at the butcher shop . . . take a number* (chuckling) *only you can take all the numbers. Just keep accepting as they come . . . accept! Accept! You are not taking anything away from anybody else. This is all lined up just for you. Feel the Love? Everybody else has their own lineup waiting for them to open up and accept. If somebody gives you something it doesn't mean that someone else will go without.*

THERE IS NO LIMIT . . . THERE IS NO LIMITATION OR SHORTAGE . . . THERE IS ONLY CREATIVE ABUNDANCE! THERE IS ONLY MORE! *Just like the pain you created in your back and your arm and your elbow and your wrist . . . through stopping the energy, holding back, blocking. When you do not accept your true* VALUE . . . *all that is coming to you, all that is lined up for you . . . just for you, you're blocking, you're stopping, you're not accepting.* ACCEPT.

Anthony is on a real roll in this session about abundance using changes in tone and speed of the voice and introducing one little video after the other.

A: *Open up! Open, stop sticking your fingers in the dike* (laughing). *Let if flow . . . oh feel that glorious flow around you . . . that warm, loving flow. It's yours. It is your birthright. Abundance. Abundance. You don't need to create abundance. It's already there. In fact you can't create abundance.*

ABUNDANCE IS! ABUNDANCE IS THE NATURAL STATE! *All you can do is stop the flow. So then when you start it again, you think you're creating abundance. But you're not.* IT'S THERE! IT'S JUST THERE! IT IS PART OF CREATION. IT IS HOW IT IS! YOU DON'T HAVE TO DO ANYTHING EXCEPT STOP BLOCKING

IT'S YOUR MOVIE!

THE FLOW. START ACCEPTING.

In fact, just make a decision. Today, I will accept. I will accept whatever comes my way. I will open my arms to receive it, embrace it, and run with it! And do that every day, every day, and soon you'll forget. You won't even know how to block it. It will be done . . . start today! Open up! Welcome it! Sing to it . . . like that birdie on the branch . . . Yes . . . it's all it is really . . . it's all it is. YOU ARE HEALING, LOVING, EXPANSIVE LIGHT! THAT IS WHAT YOU ARE! IT MATTERS NOT HOW YOU CHOOSE TO USE THAT HEALING, LOVING, EXPANSIVE LIGHT.

Here Anthony is showing me little videos of a watering hose and the train.

A: You can do it in a number of ways. Have fun with it. Help your brothers and sisters but don't put pressure on yourself, because just like a hose, where you put pressure you block, and when you block, you stop the flow. You don't really stop the flow, because it's still there, it's still there, it doesn't go away, you just block it, you close it off, close if off, it builds up pressure . . . a head of steam, just like your train. It builds up a head of steam and all you need to do is take off the brake and away you go again.

It's just that easy. There's nothing complicated. There are no big algorithms and theories and formulae. It's just that easy. LOVE IS, ALWAYS WILL BE. AND YOU ARE LOVE, ALWAYS WILL BE! LOVE HEALS! Pretty simple stuff . . . pretty simple stuff. And now, my love, time to go.

Summary Notes:

When Anthony says "what goes in comes out" he is referring to a bird's digestive system. I had been reading a few days before (After a bird pooped on the seat of my golf cart) about how birds did not have "holding tanks" so to speak. What they eat gets immediately digested and the waste is let go.

CHAPTER 13:
WEEK TWO

Sixth Channel—February 14, 2013

This day before sitting down to channel, I had been reading emails, looking at Facebook, and searching on YouTube. On Facebook, I read a post that described the energy power of the pyramid shape and talked about research done in Russia by various academic and medical groups. The research was described as being sound and scientific. Studies and results were listed. And, then I browsed the comments . . . some pro, some anti, some attacking the pros, some attacking the antis. I had a slight urge to check out some of the pro and anti statements by doing my own research, but I decided instead to search YouTube to find the video I had listened to before going to bed last night. It was an activation by someone channeling messages from the Pleiades.

I didn't find that video, but I did find a message about Star Seeds and how to tell if you are one. I watched the video and the mention of sensitivities and food allergies caught my attention. Many in my family, including me, have food sensitivities and allergies. I pondered that for a bit before spotting a video of Esther Hicks channeling Abraham. It had been some time since I had listened to Abraham and I was moved to watch. The similarity between this Abraham message and other "newer" messages I had been hearing surprised me. I had been told that Abraham's message was a bit behind the times. It was just after watching this video that I settled in to channel Anthony.

The recording is 41 minutes. There are only breathing sounds until 4 minutes then a bit of coughing and Anthony started talking.

Paraphrased message:

This is such a long and rambling message that if I were to have received it as a third party, I would be a little confused about what the message really is. So here goes, my best attempt. "Your guides say you have some questions about food allergies. Do not resist or try to fix things related to food and its production. Listen to your body, it will tell you what it wants. You are uncomfortable being a leader and you are uncomfortable being a follower. You are looking for a model of cooperation that resonates with you. You will find it by connecting to your higher levels. Resisting or fighting against something brings the energy down. Do not resist and do not worry about the opinions of others or judge them."

Here are Anthony's words.

A: It won't always be this way you know. You think it takes a long time so it does. No matter. What is time anyway? Just a fig-a-ment. (chuckle)

IT'S YOUR MOVIE!

Anthony was referring to the time it takes for him to come through. I had been wondering if we could speed up the process or make it so there was no "process."

A: You wanted to know today about food and allergies. You already understand a good deal of that. It's all energy, you know that. You get frustrated with yourself because you cannot use your mind to convince your body that it's just bits of light energy and it can use it or not. Your mind (chuckle), *it's a wonderful tool, smart* (laughing), *but only the little ego could possibly think that the mind could direct consciousness . . . only the little ego.*

It's there, you know . . . your true ability. You know what it is. It's so hard on you, the energy of manipulation and financial violence that surrounds and infuses all those poor little seeds and follows all the way through . . . the grinding and the spraying and all those things . . . follows all the way through. It's not the label, it's not the gluten, it's the violence the violence committed on those poor little seeds. WE DON'T LIKE HOW YOU ARE SO WE'LL CHANGE YOU.

They were perfect. They were perfect, just like you're perfect. There was no need to change them . . . no need. How do you deal with it now? You just accept it. It's that easy. Don't fight against it, don't criticize it, don't complain about it, don't avoid it just accept it—accept it!

Your body will naturally ask you for what it needs; give it to it. But remember, your body is your vehicle . . . you can use it for PLEASURE too! It's not just to get you from here to there! To help you speak and hear and see . . . no . . . it's for pleasure. Use it for pleasure! Things taste good . . . enjoy it! Enjoy it! Let yourself enjoy it! Go ahead . . . go ahead.

PATRICIA McHUGH

It's a book day. You saw the pyramid thing. You saw the comments. Use that. Use that today. There's truth in it . . . it's covered. Tell them . . . tell them these things exist . . . but it's people looking outside of themselves for the answers. That energy is the same energy that's accessible to all. You are a pillar of light. They are pillars of light. They don't need a pyramid to attract the energy to themselves or to use it, but it will help. It's a stepping stone, just like the light bulb, just like the discovery of e-lec-tric-ity (chuckle). *It's funny how you call it that . . . figure out all the different kinds and label them and work with them . . . it's all part of the game, you'll get there* (laughter) *and when you get to the end and realize, when you really, really realize, you will think . . . holy smoley . . . those are your words, I've heard you use them . . . holy smoley, why didn't we just go direct, just plug in?* (laughing as talking)

But that's half the fun . . . the creating, the playing, you see. You know . . . everybody knows . . . you've all seen it, the beautiful, pink energy . . . the effortlessness of creation . . . you've seen it (chuckle). *You just forgot, and so you keep trying, keep trying and you throw in all your other little game rules like . . . I gotta be there first, and I gotta protect mine and I gotta make more money from it than you and don't you use it it's mine, no, I found it it's mine . . . finders keepers, losers weepers. I don't want to play with you because you don't have enough, you're not smart enough, you're raggy. I want to play with them because they have more, they can get something for me . . .* (chuckle) *all part of the game, all part of the game . . . like Mexican train. I put up my train when I want you to help me . . . and you can help yourself at the same time. And then whoa, oh, oh, I take down my train and you can't play with me anymore . . . you have to do it yourself . . . oh, okay, now we can share again . . . oh no no, not now cause I'm ahead.*

That's how it is; doesn't have to be that way, but that's how it is, because

IT'S YOUR MOVIE!

that's the game, the game of life on Earth the way most people see it, the way most people play it, and if you don't, you're not in the game. So then what do you do? Do you sit by yourself and talk to hummingbirds? Or listen to music, or find other people just like you and try to keep connected with them? Sure . . . new game, new game called . . . I don't play with you guys cause I don't like your rules. Okay, new game . . . new game is nobody can make any rules . . . don't make any rules 'cause then I'm not going to play . . . love me, I'll love you, have fun, be happy, okay, and then what? Then what?

Well . . . okay, let's all go help the world, okay, that'll be our new game. We're not playing their old game. We don't like the rules, so we're having a new game. The new game is called "Let's all go help the world" . . . alright . . . cause we're more loving, we're better. Now, should we all help the world the same way? No because I'm a little better helper than you and so I'm going to do it this way . . . and uh, I'll teach you how to do it this way . . . if you give me money. Now I don't know where you're going to get the money from. Just know that it'll come. Okay? Just know that it'll come . . . and then you can pay me to show you how to help. There are other people over there helping too, but I think my way's a little better, but if you like that way, go ahead . . . but I really think my way's a little better so just, uh, okay, we'll make it a little less money, but uh, yeah I'll teach you how to help . . . mmm then what?

Feels the same? Feels nicer, feels like helping is a better game than getting. And you're right (laughter) *and you're wrong* (laughter) *and you're you. So how do you do it, then? That's your question, isn't it . . . it feels like . . . different and it feels like . . . you know . . . moving on up . . . but then it feels the same. So how you gonna do it?*

This was a long piece of the message and my mind was starting to wander (perhaps I should say *wonder*—as in *wonder where this is going?*) so Anthony is asking me to get my head out of the way again.

A: Get your head out of the way! Stop determining good/better/best (chuckle). *We should have called you Censor. You don't need to censor. It's all part of the holding yourself too tight, trying to figure out if it's right or wrong, good or bad, or better or worse. Just go with it. Lean in as your friend Jennifer says. You see, the thing is, you see it as following. If you listen to this one, you're FOLLOWING this one. If you listen to that one, you're FOLLOWING that one.*

It appears we are not yet finished with this topic and Anthony is going to try a video.

A: You see that path up that mountain? It's comfortable to be a follower because somebody has already checked out the way ahead, has found the way. But what's the fun in that . . . trudging along, nose to tail, (chuckle) *face to bum . . . eyes down, watch your step . . . follow, Oh STOP, stop ahead . . . okay, we can go . . . what's the fun in that?*

We keep telling you, you're here to have fun. You know that I hear the words coming out of your mouth all the time. You tell your dollies, you tell your friends. Have fun. So what's the fun in that?

Okay, round up your own team, be the leader, the one with the biggest stick. "Alright, look ahead, oh, keep an eye out, oh, what's that? Are they all okay back behind? Oh, that one has asthma, is she gonna be okay? Are they gonna want to do this again, will they pay me to do this again? Oh, I'd better make it more fun, how am I gonna make it more fun?" Oh . . .Is this fun? Is this better? You're not following. You're in charge. Maybe feels a little different . . . maybe you get a little more amped up. But is it

IT'S YOUR MOVIE!

fun? Is it fun? Didn't think so. So now what?

It's no fun to be the leader, it's no fun to be the follower, and there are no examples, real good examples of working together. That's what you've really been looking for, isn't it . . . some kind of connection . . . like those birds in the big flocks that fly and swoop and adjust. Or those fish in the schools . . . all going together . . . that kind of connection. You know where you find that? Plugging in. Tapping in to your true source . . . the one true source . . . and then what? And then what? You're floating, that's what . . . just waiting . . . waiting

Anthony has started singing and brings in the train.

A: I see the train a comin', comin' down the track . . . Waiting . . . is that any fun? Feels good for awhile but then you might as well not be there in the physical plane. But you are, and you're there for a very good reason. You're there to help the planet evolve . . . to grow . . . to expand . . . to create. And, you don't do that by fighting. You have a strong resistance to FIGHTING. You can't understand why people are intrigued with war or why they want to watch people fight each other.

There are different kinds of fighting. Fighting is resistance. If you're fighting for something you think is good . . . is that different? Just because you're fighting for something you think is good? It's fighting . . . it's resistance.

You know what happens when you put a resistor into one of your e-lec-tric-al circuits? It dampens down the energy. Does it matter if it's a black resistor or a white resistor or a yellow resistor or a pink resistor? Or if the company that created it was full of love and bubbles or was just after the money? Does it matter? No. It's a resistor. It dampens the energy.

You are here to receive and transmit . . . to increase the vibrational frequency of the planet. You're one of many and that's your job. And you can't do that . . . as well . . . (chuckle) you can still do it. You know that. You've done that, bull through, keep going, get up, start again, tough it out, wait it out, threaten a little, use a carrot, use a stick, you've done all that . . . but it wasn't enough was it? You know there's more. Pull the plug! Take out the resistor, open it up, let it flow, feel it.

Don't worry about what the new rules are. You're really good with those words . . . forget them . . . go with the flow. Resistance is resistance. Let it go! Let it go! Let it go! Don't let it burn out the filament. Let it shine. You don't need to understand it, or research it, or read those things or those comments and figure out who's right and who's wrong. It doesn't matter. IT JUST DOESN'T MATTER.

Anthony was referring to the Facebook post and the comments I had been reading that morning before we opened the channel.

A: There will be heaven on Earth. You can't see it from there. Just keep moving. Keep moving . . . shine the light forward. You'll see more and more as it opens up in front of you like a beautiful, beautiful flower . . . expanding, GLOWING, warm, welcoming beacon. Move toward it! Just go. Just go!

It was time for a break in the action, so Anthony started singing and brought in the train. It's almost like he is saying, "I've given you a lot to think about today and it's now time for some relaxation." He loves this train visual and is always playful when it comes in.

A: Here it comes (singing) *I hear the train a comin', comin' down the track . . . All Aboard* (chuckle) *. . . see the conductor with his big smile*

IT'S YOUR MOVIE!

and his bright blue hat? Get on, sit down, and enjoy the ride...'BOARD ... (chuckle)

Summary Notes:

Mexican Train is a board game played with special dominoes and the object is to be the first to place all your dominoes. The rules allow for individual play where you are the only one allowed to put dominoes down on your own "train" and team play where you let the other players play on your train. I'm not surprised that Anthony used this analogy. He seems to love trains.

This is the first of several messages that circle the topic of competition. This has been a big one for me. After spending three decades with my head down and nose to the grindstone in the competitive business world, I was now searching for something I thought was better. And I was watching closely to what I perceived was happening in the spiritual enlightenment "industry." Much of the rambling message today revolved around that topic. It will likely seem like a lot of rambling gobbledygook to you, but it carried a pretty deep and thought-provoking message for me. This is another example of the beauty of personalized channels.

As I was listening to the recording, transcribing it, I so wished you could hear the voice and feel the love and playfulness as it came through. And then it dawned on me. You can. All you have to do is open a channel your own guide.

PATRICIA McHUGH

Seventh Channel—February 15, 2013

It was 1:30 in the afternoon and I had been up since 6:00 a.m., driven one hour to the airport on a busy freeway and then one hour back home again, finished three loads of laundry, chopped vegetables, and made a stir fry for lunch, and put bread on to bake. My body was tired and achy and I was feeling guilty because I hadn't figured out how to fix it, to make it perfectly healthy. This was the frame of mind in which I sat down to channel Anthony. Not surprisingly, my question was "What is real about this body thing? Does what I eat have anything to do with it? Can I heal it? Can I heal other people?"

At the same time, the neighbors had landscapers in their yard pruning a big tree with a chain saw. I was feeling for the tree, wondering if they had talked nicely to it before starting, if it was really necessary, if it was a "bad" thing to do.

As I was relaxing in the session, I realized that I do it with my eyes closed and I had seen other people channeling with their eyes open. So in addition to the questions about my physicality and healing abilities, I was asking Anthony if I could just immediately open the channel, channel with my eyes open, and have him answer questions for other people as well as for me.

The channel was relatively easy to open. It took only 3 minutes for the talking to start.

Paraphrased message:

I would explain this message to myself in this way: "You can channel

IT'S YOUR MOVIE!

in whichever way you want and you can channel for yourself or someone else. Eyes open, eyes closed, it does not matter. The less you worry about it the easier it will be. You want to heal other people to help them and you also want to heal other people to help yourself, to prove to yourself that you can do it. You can heal yourself and other people by being the channel through which healing is offered but you are limiting the possibilities by trying to be in control of the process. You are somewhat attached to the discomforts you produce in your body and have a strong tendency to relate them directly to what you eat because it gives you a feeling of safety and of being in control. Your guide says it is difficult to find the right words to answer your questions about healing and health."

These are Anthony's words.

A: Yes you can. You can do it any way you want. I told you yesterday, it doesn't have to be difficult. You'll get used to it. You'll get over worrying about whether or not you can do it and if it's real. You'll get used to it and then you'll just do it however you want . . . eyes open, eyes closed, your own questions or someone else's. However you want.

Anthony answered my questions about opening the channel and moved on to the topic of health. He started by mimicking my thoughts and having a little laugh at me and then tried to explain again his earlier message that they could heal my body and all I had to do was approve.

A: You're still on the body thing . . . still wanting to know . . . still very much tied into it. (chuckle) trying to run it, control it. That's why you want to know . . . so you can be in charge. Hum . . . if I feed it this will it feel good? If I do that will it feel good? Do I need to do this exercise on this schedule? Will that make it feel better? How am I going to get rid of this joint pain? (laughing) *I told you we could do it and all you had to do was approve. I didn't mean all you had to do was approve that it could be done, or whether or not you wanted it done. I meant approve "we can do it"... that means you have to get out of the way. That means "we" do it, not you do it!*

Anthony then went on to discuss the "yeah, buts" he knew were swirling in my mind. The message that I like to be in charge, to control, is not a new one. And it was not a surprise to me. It seemed that on one level I wanted to know the rules so that I could predict the outcome based on my actions.

A: Yes, I know you feel those direct correlations. When you eat this, you feel that, when you don't exercise you feel that, when you do this you feel that. Umhmm ... Is it real? That's what you want to know ... or are you just doing it? Sort of like, if I poke him, I know what he's going to do, or, if I disagree with her, I know what she's going to do. That means "I'm in charge" so then, if I don't want him to do that, I don't poke him, or if I don't want her to do that, I don't disagree.

That's how you think isn't it? You're going to be in charge. You're going to control the behavior of the people around you. Why are you doing that? Why do you need to control that? What are you afraid of? Are you afraid if you let go—what? WHAT? You'll just fly off the end of the Earth? (chuckle) *What, what are you afraid of? Why do you want to do that? I know you want to help people, I know you'd like to heal them ... be in charge.*

Anthony loves to have a chuckle, and here he is having fun over the idea of fairness or unfairness. It is just another example of the duality of judgment that we humans have created and which Anthony thinks is funny.

A: No maybe that's a little unfair (chuckle) *... or fair. You can do that, you know. You can do anything, anything, as long as you do it for the right reasons. If you're trying to control, you can't do it ... trying to control how other people deal with their own body issues—here, let me fix you the nice way so you don't have to go through any of those icky ways, those invasive ways, those bad people ways. Let me do it nicely, so you don't have to suffer, so everything's nice, so everybody's comfortable.*

It's sort of like a bad apple. If there's one bad apple in the bin, they all go bad. So if you can heal all those other people in a nice way, then everybody's healed, and you will be too. But if you have people around you that are broken physically and can't be fixed ... bad apples with rotten bits that means you might be like that too, maybe you can't be fixed. Makes you vulnerable. You don't like to be vulnerable.

Anthony then explained to me a little bit more about how healing occurs. It seems as though Anthony is juggling the word symbols again. Sometimes "you" means the bigger me, and sometimes "you" means the little me, the part I most often think about as me, the part that lives in my physical body.

A: You CAN heal people. You can heal yourself ... with our help of course. You can be the channel, the healing channel. Will that help you to accept, to lose the fear, to go with the flow ... to fly? It's a noble calling, to heal the physical body. It is. If it helps those people to remember who they really are and to raise their own vibrational frequencies so that we can help the planet, then that's one thing.

Here Anthony referred to the books and things I have seen and heard about how our thoughts and emotions cause disease and discomfort in our physical bodies, and he is trying to find the words to help me understand. I was also distracted by the chainsaw noise in the neighbors' yard, and our connection was growing weak. I finally became too distracted to continue and the connection was dropped.

A: I know you still wonder. You wonder why do they get sick, why do you get sick? You hear it . . . you cause it, thoughts, emotions and all of those words and logic. There's a little bit of everything involved, a little bit of all of it. It's a hard one. It's a hard one to say in your words. It's a hard one. You don't like the pain. You don't like the limitations. Don't eat this or you'll feel that. Don't sit down all day or you'll get fat and you'll feel this and you'll look like that. It's a hard one.

By "*it's a hard one,*" Anthony means it is a hard one to put into words.

Summary Notes:

The main topic in this message, healing and health, is one that has occupied my thoughts for many years. Perhaps it was the distraction from the chainsaw next door that caused the channel to drop that morning. Perhaps it was the level of emotion I feel around the subject. Perhaps it was a combination of the two. In any case, I was somewhat disappointed and hoped that Anthony would pick up this topic again.

IT'S YOUR MOVIE!

Eighth Channel—February 16, 2013

As I prepared for a formal channel session, I didn't have a specific question. I just asked for "something new."

Although it felt like about five minutes while I was doing it, the total time on my recorder was 31 minutes. I started some meditative breathing and soon Anthony began clearing my throat and getting the channel ready. He started talking at 4:45 minutes.

Paraphrased message:

I identified three main themes in this message. They are *fun*, *fear*, and *accomplishment*, and I would explain them like this. "The ideas you have come from the bigger you. Life is just like a big amusement park. It is all fun until you start to take it too seriously. It is taking it too seriously that stops you from carrying through with ideas you have for doing things you would enjoy. You feel that you have to be doing something important, something to save the world, but you don't. Your job is to have fun. Your physical breathing problems stem from fear. You are concerned about the problems humanity is creating for the Earth and want to do something about it. Do not get involved in fighting against these things. Choose an idea and move toward it. This will help to raise the vibration of the planet and will do more to help the people of the Earth than fighting for a cause."

Here are Anthony's words:

A: Okay, okay, I will. I'll give you something you don't know . . . but actually you know ... that the things you have thought of have come from me too ... and you ... we.

Anthony is using a video analogy of a roller coaster to describe my pattern of getting excited about something, not following through, and then feeling bummed.

A: Yes, it's like a roller coaster. You see the roller coaster? Wooo ... Yeah, as you come down it's exhilarating, and then wooooo ... you're racing up the other side ... hovering at the top ... waiting ... and then you're down, and around, and up and down and it screeches to a stop, and you get out, and you say—wowser, I don't wanna do that again! But then you do ... then you do.

Anthony is having a bit of fun here with the word "wowser." It is something I often say. He then goes on to explain to me what it is about this cycle of getting excited, not following through, and then getting bummed. He is also having a bit of fun with the word "normal."

A: It's the adrenaline rush, you know ... and then when it stops, it just feels empty. It just feels empty. So then you want another one. Yes, it's normal, it's normal (chuckle) *whatever that is...*

See the cotton candy, pink and blue, and the kiddies laughing and the balloons and the sounds? It's all a big carnival. That's all it is, you know, just one big wonderland ... yeah, it's all fun, it's meant to be ... until you take it too seriously and start to monkey with it. It's like the Earth, you know, full of so many wonderful, beautiful, fun things ... until you start to monkey with it.

IT'S YOUR MOVIE!

Here Anthony switched to a video of a jungle with monkeys and birds as he once again heads down the road of control and fear.

A: You see that monkey swinging on those vines? (chuckle) *There's a whole bunch of them. See them? The rainforest... the rainforest... it's a necessary part of your world, of Earth. Yes, it's like the lungs, like Earth's lungs. It's breathing out what you're breathing in. It's the oxygen factor you see. It's designed that way. You need it, that's the one thing you can't do without. You can do without food, you can do without water, but you can't do without oxygen. You feel that acutely ... the breathing thing. It's one of your issues* (laughing) *... you and your lungs, your physical lungs, one of your issues that you will solve, that you will clear ... not by figuring it out ... by letting it go.* (Here Anthony has a heavy sigh.) *Letting it go ... it's a fear thing, you know, like so many of your things in your physical body. It's a fear thing.*

See that bird? It's a mynah bird ... has some of your qualities, some of the same qualities. Yeah ... it's not a malady you know, or short coming or a downfall, your fear thing. It's part of the Earth experience. It's built into so many things.

The movie in the channel has changed and is now showing me scenes involving animals from my experiences in daily life in Arizona and in Canada as Anthony continues to talk about fear.

A: Look at the animal kingdom ... drive by those bunnies on the street in your golf cart and they run, they're frightened ... the quail, running and running to get away from the noise and the tires of the golf cart. They're frightened. The difference is they're not frightened all the time. They keep their senses alert, they have their noses and their ears tuned, but they don't react until it's necessary. They don't hold their bodies tight all the time.

You see those deer, how they spring up and bound away ... and moments before they were chewing on the grass and lying on the ground. That's the difference, you know. The difference is they only do it when they need to do it. The difference is they don't go to this blade of grass and say, hmmm ... now if I eat too many blades of this grass will my tummy hurt? No, they just go with what they know. They just know ... those berries are poisonous ... they just know.

Now we are going back to a subject Anthony talked about a few days earlier—food and how it affects me; Anthony is changing the message a bit from the last time.

A: It's not the food, you know, it's the contemplation. It's not even really the energy attached to the food. No, that's ... that's just something more to be afraid of ... a new unknown. Where did this come from? What's attached to it? How do I change the energy of this? No ... don't go there, don't go there.

I know you see the problems. You see what's happening, you see how your humanity is treating your Earth ... and it hurts and you're conflicted. If you get involved in a fight to save the planet, then that's a fight, and you really don't like fights. And if you don't get involved in a fight to save the planet, then how's it going to get saved? If you don't do it, how's it going to get done?

Back to that one again ... and yet, if you just sit on the sidelines blowing bubbles and waving at birdies, what's the point in being here? Why be there? You keep coming back to the hard, hard ones ... what's the right thing to do? And you know there's no right thing and there's no wrong *thing, there's no thing . . . and yet you want to contribute, you want to do something **meaningful**, something **helpful**.* (Anthony emphasized those words.) *At bottom, most do . . . most do.*

Anthony has switched from fear to another of his favorite topics—judgment.

*A: So here's one, clearer, more concise—what is the best thing to do? No different really is it from what is the right thing to do? It still snags on you. It still doesn't feel right. So what can you do? What can you do? **Maintain, sustain,** (chuckle) perchance to dream?*

Something different happened here at this point on this recording. The voice had a questioning tone and Anthony seemed to be searching and trying out different words. The next words (the ones in bold.) were said with emphasis as though Anthony wanted to hear what they sounded like and see if they were a fit for what he was trying to get across. And then he seemed to have found a way to continue with the message when he came to the word "well." During this time there was no video to go with the words, but then it came again when he started talking about the women at the well.

*A: **Sustenance, manna, nourish, nurture, feed, gather, prepare, wish them well** . . . See the ladies at the well hauling water . . . miles and miles a day . . . and the girls . . . breaks your heart. Raise the vibrational frequency! Catch the ideas that are out there in the ethers! Expand on them grow them! Nurture them! Help them unfold. Write about them. They're all out there. They're out there floating around waiting for someone to pick them, to pick them, to be attracted to them, to unfold them, display them . . . for all the world to see. No matter if people like them or make fun of them or fight against them . . . no matter. Because* *once they're out, they're there ... they're there! They're anchored. They're placed. They move it up a notch and no amount of disagreement or hate can move it back down.*

Here Anthony was showing me an image of a cloudy, veil-like ceiling above the Earth that limited the energy field. There was an area above this ceiling in which ideas were placed and they floated in that space. The voice emphasized the words that are in bold and it was almost as though he was excited to have landed on an analogy that could get his message across.

A: Raise the ceiling. **That's what you need to do! Raise the ceiling!** *Don't try to make people quit doing things or resist them or refuse them or boycott them—raise the ceiling! Ratchet it up! Grab those ideas, pull them through and open them up, they let loose the power ... something like hydraulics ... it increases the pressure and pushes the ceiling up. Once it's raised, it can't come back down. It's there.*

And now we were back to seeing the ladies and the girls carrying water. They looked happier and their steps were lighter because the energy had been raised.

A: You see those ladies and those girls? Their loads are lighter. They're beginning to see and to understand just how powerful they really are. You see those red ladies, those ladies in red in India? They have an idea of how powerful they are. They're powerful when they band together with their sticks. They will come to know how powerful they are standing as one, alone with no stick. That's the way to do it. Stand alone together with no stick, knowing, knowing your power ... raising the frequency, lifting the ceiling, expanding the true nature of who you really are ... joining the clouds ... flying. I've told you before you can fly. You have a real interest in flying. You will fly. You will fly! It's a vibratory frequency thing.

Anthony then moved to a different visual. He never stays too long on one video because my mind gets involved and muddies the channel.

A: *Hear the bell? You see that bell, that big iron bell? Look at it. See it vibrating? Hear the sound it makes? It's a freedom bell.*

Here Anthony began singing softly. The train was arriving and it was time to end the session.

A: *I hear that train a comin', comin' down the track. Here it comes, here it comes ... time to get on and go to the next station. Settle in, and watch the beautiful scenery.*

Summary Notes:

The red ladies in India that Anthony referred to are called the Red Brigade. The Brigade is a growing group of women in India, many of whom who have been the victim of sexual violence, who have banded together to fight for and protect women. These women train in martial arts and present a united and retaliatory front to prevent and avenge abuse against women.

Ninth Channel—February 18, 2013

We seemed to have settled into a routine where I would set my intention to channel, relax my body and start the breathing and visualization technique I had developed. At the same time, Anthony would be doing his thing, getting my body ready to start speaking. The time on the recording was 39 minutes and Anthony started talking after four minutes. During those minutes, Anthony was showing me images and whispering to me to get my mental chatter out of the way and encourage me to open up so he could speak.

This was the strongest channel yet, the one where I felt the most physical connection. It was emotional and filled with physical sensations and movements. My hands were cradling a ball of energy, being moved, feeling, sensing, and there were silent tears running down my face. The message also started differently. Instead of showing me the train or another visual or trying to jolly my mind out of the way, Anthony came in announcing who he was. It felt like he had taken over my body more than had happened in the past.

Paraphrased message:

This channel session made me realize even more fully the value of opening your own channel. There is no way for a third party to give you the full experience, the physical sensations, the emotions, the tones of voice. There is no way to translate the earnestness with which Anthony tried to get across a message that our words cannot explain and for which there is no physical framework. The best I could do would be something like this: "Your guide says you are still playing the game of life the way you developed it and it won't work. He says you can see the parts you don't like and make adjustments to the rules or pretend you aren't playing the game to make yourself feel better but it is a no-win game and it won't work. There is a game. It is the game developed by God and you knew the rules before you came to Earth. He is saying that you need to change your habits, stop trying to control or look or be better. You won't find the rules for the real game in books or on the Internet. He says you knew the game and you need to remember it and you can do that by opening up and letting it come through. He says there are no words for him to be able to use to describe the game because we have only developed words for what we can see and we can't see the creation game. He is asking you to put your game away and let them teach you how to play the game you came here to play by opening up and receiving it at an inside/cellular level."

These are Anthony's words:

A: I ... aammm ... Annthony. I am Anthony.

After making his announcement, Anthony showed me a lily pad and told me to just go and sit on it—relax and get out of the way. He told me he would be in my body for a while and I should just float and go along.

A: Umhum ... it is a beautiful flower, and lily pad. You go and sit over there for a while, just float and relax. See the bee? Just settle in, float and relax. Just settle in. We'll go for a little ride today. We can't go too far 'cause that lily pad is anchored ... just like you're anchored to your Earth in some ways, some physical ways but you can still float. You can still go and float and drift and see. You can see ... not with your physical eyes, you don't need them right now. Just see ... relax. Relax and be. Relax and see ... and float and float. There you go. It's hard for me to work around you ... when you're here, still in here, so you just float over there. Yeesss, and I'll be in here for now, just for now. We have a story to tell, a story to tell. Go ahead and float, go ahead and float. There are so *many things going through your mind . . . governments and all the new ideas, but somebody already picked that one, so how am I going to find a new one? So those are the things, aren't they . . . going through your head? Yes, that's why I want you to float.*

Once Anthony has me out of the way on the lily pad, he begins to explain to me why I am feeling uncomfortable and how the game of life I have designed for myself won't work.

A: You're still in the game, that game you play, you're still in it. That game won't work! It won't work for you. It's a no-win game. It's a game that just goes around and around and around. Sure, you can change the rules . . . you know, make it seem a little easier (chuckling), *fool yourself . . . even can fool yourself into thinking you're not playing the game anymore, but you are. You just make a little a-just-ment, just change the rules a bit, change the board, and change the players. It's still the same game. Pack it up, pack that game up in the box it came in and put it away. You don't need to burn it, or bury it, or any of those things.*

Here I believe Anthony was referring to the processes I had been reading about for releasing limiting beliefs and unlocking potential. These processes had little rituals attached like writing things down and then releasing them by burning or burying, etc. He is also reminding me of times from my past when I was trying to quit smoking.

A: There's no system or right way or . . . oh, oh the boogey man's going to get you. You see, that's all just part of the game, just part of the game, just put the game away. Like when you used to smoke and you knew that your friend had some cigarettes hidden up in her closet, her front hall closet in her apartment and you had a key and you could sneak home at lunch and have one. Didn't work, did it? No. Or you threw them away.

IT'S YOUR MOVIE!

Didn't work either. It worked when you decided to just put them away . . . they just weren't what you were doing anymore. You saw yourself as a non-smoker and you became one.

Stop playing the game, DO NOT PLAY THE GAME! I know that sounds simple and it's not. If you don't play . . . you're soooo used to playing that game, what will you do? I hear it. I hear that. What was the other thing you did when you quit smoking? You changed your habits. You quit drinking coffee and you didn't sit down as much (chuckling). *You didn't even go to the lake because you associated the deck with smoking. It was worth it, wasn't it? Change your habits! Change your habits! Controlling your mind is part of the game . . . sure. Yeah . . . taking notice . . . you're beginning to notice you're playing the game and trying to control your mind is part of playing the game. Change your habits. Change your habits!*

This was a long bit of talking and my mind was starting to wander, so Anthony introduced a visual of a bird. This was not just a random bird. It was the hummingbird that had adopted our feeder and with whom I interacted regularly. I called him Humphrey (a play on Hum-free). Humphrey seems to come whenever I go outside or call him in my mind. Anthony is calling me out on trying to control and worrying about this interaction with Humphrey instead of just going with it.

A: Oh, look at that bird. Yes, he's loving you too. Isn't that nice. Doesn't come from outside you, you know. I see you get a bit ner-vous when you go outside and call him and he doesn't come . . . right away . . . in your timing. I see you . . . worrying. Maybe it's not real. Maybe I can't create. Maybe there is no com-unication between me and the bird. I hear you. It's a control thing too. It's part of the game, part of the game. Change your habits.

Change of subject again. Anthony now brings up bicycles. For the last little while I had been thinking about getting a bike and thinking it would be a good way to get into better physical shape. When I was in my 30s I had ridden a bike several miles every day.

A: You're attracted to those bicycles, aren't you? You did that once before, many years ago ... for exercise ... part of the game ... the part that was—maybe if I have a better-looking body, I'll feel better about myself. Worked to an extent too, didn't it? That's part of the game ... good/ better/best ... measuring. It's all part of the game. How well am I doing? Am I better than her, them? Did I win? Am I going to the next level? Am I asc-ending? It's all part of the game. It's all part of the game

I know you really want to GET IT, to move on, to stop playing the game, but you're still stuck in that place where you need to see what it looks like over there before you can leave where you are. That's how you did it with the smoking thing, isn't it? You became a non-smoker because in your mind you could see what that looked like. In your mind, you can't see what it looks like to not play the game. So you're finding it hard to get there. You don't know what habits to change, what habits will be outside the game. You know if you make new habits it's just changing the rules of the game. You can't see how to be. You can't see how to be because you're looking for the pattern.

The day before this channel session I had been talking with a neighbor and she was lavishing praise on a friend of hers who could sew anything you wanted.

A: You can't sew that dress without a pattern, even if you're very creative.

IT'S YOUR MOVIE!

You heard that, didn't you? Yesterday . . . She was an amazing seamstress. Amazing—she could just see any dress or you could just tell her what you wanted . . . she could go home and make a pattern and make it for you.

The pattern, you're quite willing to change, I can see that, but you're looking for the pattern. What does it need to look like? It's the game. It's the game How Can I Be Better? What book do I need to read? Maybe there's a video? You've changed the books, grown, played the game, the game of growing. You've done it very well. You're different, and the same, still playing the game. The thing is, there has to be a game . . . there has to, or else you would just be floating on that lily pad . . . and for what?

Anthony has a hard time with the word *God*. There were gagging sounds and the word sounded as though it was being dragged out of me.

A: There is a game, there IS A GAME. (gagging sounds) *Ggggg .. OD created a game. You were created as part of his game her game . . . Aaannnd* (gagging again) *now you know there is a game . . . what I want you to do is to remember the rules of the game that you came to play! You, the little you, does not have to make up the game!*

I was experiencing quite a few physical sensations during this part of the message. My body was jerking and buzzing.

A: *You came in knowing . . . REMEMBER! YOU CAME IN KNOWING. REMEMBER THE GAME! REMEMBER! YOU WON'T FIND IT IN BOOKS AND VIDEOS ON YOUR COMPUTERS. YOU WILL NOT FIND IT THERE! OPEN UP . . . OPEN UP! OPEN UP! LET IT COME! LET IT COME! LET IT COME!*

Here there was a long silence with breathing and soft sighing sounds. My body was tingling and buzzing. After a minute or two Anthony resumed in a quiet voice.

A: That's how we need to do it. It's nothing you've heard, it's nothing you've seen, there are no words for it . . . some that try . . . yes that one . . . assimilate, assimilate, catch, revolve, re . . . fold, re . . . re . . . e . . . ceive . . . receive . . . receive . . . ahhh (here there was soft sighing).

I was feeling my body opening up, tingling, a warm, loving feeling.

A: Yes . . . yes. Ohhhh . . . the day you were born doesn't matter . . . the Earth bit this time. The magnificence is the day you were created. You are you, you know . . . and yet you're not. I am you and you are me and together we are we. You can feel it. You can sense it. You can see it in your own way. That's what the yearning really is. The yearning is for the love that was the creation. Before, you were love, and then you felt love. That was the creation. You were love and then you felt love. That is the only difference. You were love, the big love, and then you were given the gift— the gift of knowing love. The words aren't there but you see, don't you? There is a game. There IS a game. It's a game called love. It's a game called remember the day you felt the love . . . even that's hard because it wasn't really a day. And you still want to do something . . . and you can. You can do love.

Put your game away and we'll teach you how to play the game you came here to play. Put yours away, pack it all up, put it in that box . . . put it away. Play . . . just play. Get your head out of the way and just play. Feel us, feel us . . . we're there . . . right there . . . guiding you . . . being you. We're right there. We're right there. Relax and let us in. We're right there. Hear us . . . not with your ears.

IT'S YOUR MOVIE!

Anthony then referred to telomeres, the tiny receivers on the end of the chromosomes in our DNA that are in constant communication with other cells in the body and with "something" outside of the body. I had recently learned that science can explain only 85-90% of the communication of telomeres. The rest is with something science cannot yet explain.

A: Yes, they gave them that name "telomeres." Hear us, catch us, receive us, you don't have to do anything really because it's already there. Just don't block us. Just open . . . open . . . open . . . aahhhhh

Summary Notes:

Anthony could see my growing discomfort with the world as I knew it. I was growing uncomfortable with the game of life I was playing. The things I had stood up for, the systems, the governments, the business rules all seemed to be less defensible. I was in limbo, wanting to move away from those things I had held true but not being able to entirely let go because I couldn't see anything that was truly better. I was trying to figure it out with my left brain the part that wanted to be able to see the whole picture and to make it all fit.

Anthony was struggling with this logical part of my mind trying to find ways to help me assimilate information in ways other than those with which I was familiar: words, things I could see with my physical eyes or visualize in my mind, and what I could hear with my physical ears. He was trying to get me to forget all the comfortable ways I had developed to guide myself through this life and to open up to a new way of taking in information by using what he calls my inside eyes. I sense these as the ones that see and communicate without me even knowing it is happening. I sense it as communication for which we have no framework and therefore cannot really describe. This was no easy task. It seemed to me like doing nothing and I had made a life practice of doing something.

After the session, my body was tingling and I felt very calm and very tired. I remember thinking, *Nothing that I "know" is real. There is no reality and I am drifting and watching.*

CHAPTER 14:
WEEK THREE

A Side Trip Into a Past Life—February 23 & 24, 2013

About a month earlier, I had stumbled on a YouTube video of an interview with Dolores Cannon. In the video, Dolores talked about her experiences and what she had learned using the Quantum Healing Hypnosis Therapy (QHHT) she had developed and used over the past forty-plus years. As I watched the video, I became really interested, not only in learning how to perform QHHT, but also in having a session with Dolores. When I went to the website to see if it would be possible for me to have a session, I discovered that there was a five-year waiting list. I was disappointed but put my name on the list anyway because this was something I really wanted to experience.

A few weeks later, I learned that Dolores would be in Sacramento, California doing a weekend event. The event was called "Empowerment of Creation" and featured Dolores Cannon and Dee Wallace. Dolores would be talking about Quantum Healing

Hypnosis Therapy and the things she learned from decades of using hypnotherapy to regress people into past lives chosen by their "subconscious" to provide information and healing to help them in this lifetime. And, during the course of the weekend, Dolores would be doing a group past life regression. This wasn't a private session with Dolores but I was excited nevertheless. Sacramento, here I come!

When she regresses clients individually, Dolores has them lying comfortably on a bed with a cozy blanket and a recorder to record the session. This was a group session and we all needed to keep our butts firmly planted so we wouldn't topple over. At the same time we needed to be relaxed enough to disengage from our physical surroundings and our conscious mind.

Dolores explained what we would be doing. She would be putting us in a light trance and leading us through some visualization. We would each go to a past life chosen by our "subconsciouses" to provide us with a lesson relevant to this life.

I will give you a sense of what I saw and learned. It shows another way in which we can receive guidance and assistance from higher levels and provides background for Anthony's references to this experience in subsequent channel sessions.

The lights were dimmed and Dolores began guiding us with visualization. I had by then become quite comfortable with the "state of mind" I am in when channeling Anthony. It is a state where I am detached from my conscious mind and have been relieved of much of the control of my physical body. My eagerness and complete lack of fear, combined with Dolores Cannon's master hypnotherapist talents, allowed me to go quickly and easily into a past life "video."

IT'S YOUR MOVIE!

We were at the point where we were visualizing a doorway beyond which we would see a significant past life and Dolores was guiding us.

"What does the ground look like? What do you see?"

I saw air. There was no ground. I knew I was very high up and there was no ground. Dolores' next instruction was to walk through the doorway. I knew there was no ground but I also knew that I was not afraid. I walked through and then I flew.

"What are you wearing? Look at the clothes you are wearing."

I was wearing a beautiful sparkly emerald green costume and I had gossamer wings. I was flying (shades of Tinkerbell).

Dolores' next instruction was "Go to the place where you live; you are standing outside the place where you live. What does it look like?"

It was a funky-looking tree house thing with big window holes and a rope and board stairway to the door. Instinctively, I knew I didn't use the door. I flew in and out of the big windows.

"See the place where you prepare your meals."

I looked around the small room. There was no kitchen, no stove, no place to prepare a meal, and so I knew. I don't eat! I am nourished by the sun, by the light. The only furniture in the room was a cocoon-like hammock that seemed like my sleeping place.

"Now, see what you do to occupy your time all day. Do you work?

What kind of work do you do? Are there other people there? Are any of them people that you know in your present life? "

Well, I flew and flitted and dazzled and sprinkled and made everybody happy. That's what I did all day. I flew around and made sure everybody was happy. There were no other people, only me. The beings I was making happy were forest creatures with no recognizable form, they were not bunnies, or foxes, or forest animals I would recognize. They were just beings.

Now Dolores asked us to move to an important day in this life: "See an important day. What is happening?"

I became aware of a monk-like creature standing at the edge of the forest. I could not see a face, just a brown cowl-hooded cassock and no real shape other that the cassock. I knew he was there to watch out for me. And then the ground started to shake and rumble. Dust was rising and I could see coming over the dust the heads of huge charging horses and armored warriors. I flew and flitted and gathered and herded the beings from the forest into a tunnel and under the ground. I was guiding and encouraging, rounding them all up and telling them to "build the lattice." The lattice was a network of support webs that created room for them to move and held up the Earth above our heads. We were safe.

Dolores asked us to move forward again in that life to another important day. "What do you see?"

I was growing weaker. My wings had withered and fallen off and the forest beings were tending to my back, rubbing something on the stumps where my wings had been. I no longer needed the wings, there was no room to fly, and I was growing weaker because I needed the light for sustenance. The forest beings were finding things to eat under the ground so they were able to survive. They seemed to be blobby and mole-like in this scene. They didn't need sunshine or light.

Again Dolores asked us to move forward, this time to the last day of that life. "What do you see?"

I was lying in a small wooden bed, very weak, and the forest beings were gathering around. They could do nothing for me. I needed light and there was no light in our underground home. It was a safe place for them but a death trap for me.

Then Dolores said, "That life is now over; you have left the body. What do you see?"

I saw me back on the spirit side with my wings in place and a smile on my face. I was communicating with the underground beings, telling them it was okay for them to eat my remains, my dead body. It would provide them with sustenance and it was of no further use to me.

As she was bringing us out of the hypnotic trance, Dolores told us that we would remember everything long enough to write it down, that we were not to talk to anyone until we had written it down, and that there was a message for us in the past life experience we had seen. She also asked us to make note of any people we had seen in that past life who may be in our current lives.

As I wrote, I realized that the monk-like being was my husband in this life and that he was watching out for me. I also realized that the creatures I had worked so hard to guide into their new underground home would have survived without me. It was I who did not survive. I could have survived simply by flying away when the intruders came. I could have saved myself. I could also have helped the forest beings into their underground refuge and then saved myself by flying away. A guard watching out for me didn't save me, and putting the welfare of all the forest creatures ahead of my own didn't save me. It was up to me to save myself. I chose instead to try and save everyone else, and in the process I killed myself. By insisting on being in charge and seeing it through, I blocked off the light, my life force.

Tenth Channel—February 24, 2013

We did this channel session on the second day of the event in Sacramento and I was asking Anthony about "next steps." The time on the recorder time was 24 minutes.

Paraphrased message:

"You were created of and by God and you are here to create a joyful life experience. He says there is no right or wrong or better than or worse than. There is only love and joyful creation, and just as a child creates beautiful crafts, you can create a beautiful life. He says that there are some who can see you and others who cannot. Do not drag yourself down by using words with those who cannot see."

These are Anthony's words:

IT'S YOUR MOVIE!

A: (singing softly) I see that train a comin', coming down the track . . . puffing out a lot of smoke . . . steam (very soft voice) smoke, smoke from the coal. That's how it always has been. Carbon . . . the carbon . . . yes it contains power . . . the carbon. And if you leave it long enough, it turns to diamond. Powerfully strong material, diamonds. They have a different, much different frequency. They're much closer to light. They're involved in the grid in a different way. They are expansive. They don't drag it down or block it. They're very powerful. They need to stay in the ground to do their work.

That day, Dolores had done the group past-life regression exercise. After we finished, Dolores asked for volunteers to come up and tell about their experience. It had been a very exciting and insightful experience for me and I was inclined to tell everyone about it. I was about to raise my hand when I heard a soft voice telling me *"not now"* so I settled back and listened instead.

A: No need to speak. No need. Your power is radiating. You are a radiant being. Your voice . . . your voice is like the sun, it makes no sound, but it shines. It shines its beautiful, powerful, healing light on everybody. It makes no sound, the sun . . . it just shines. It is the center of your world. You are the center of your world . . . shine! Shine on . . . like the harvest moon. (Here Anthony is chuckling, having a bit of fun.)

I have always loved the sun. My mood is much brighter when the sun is shining and I often yearn for the warmth of the sun. Anthony never misses an opportunity to remind me of our connection with each other and with the source of all creation. I believe it is the foundation of all his messages, the most important thing for me to "get."

A: You are the sun. You wanted the sun. You have no idea, no idea. You are the sun. You are the sun and the stars. You are the one. You are the one. Shine your voice. Shine it! Yes, that's me and it's you. I am you and you are me and together we are we.

About two years prior, my daughter had given me a beautiful journal, and most days I wrote something in it. During my first winter alone in Arizona, I had been asking for friends with whom I had things in common. My daughter's psychic friend had suggested I write in my journal thanking my higher levels for bringing me new friends with whom I could see eye to eye. Within a few months my life had changed dramatically, and I had many new friends. I had been reading back pages of my journal that morning.

A: *It's all timing. You saw that in your book this morning. You asked for those friends . . . you had no idea, no idea how your world would expand, how many people you would see eye to eye with. Your eyes, they shine, they sparkle, they hit some people and not others . . . some cannot receive . . . some are like those mole people.* (Anthony is referring to the creatures I saw during the past life regression Dolores Cannon did with the group.) *They cannot see. They cannot see!*

Here Anthony starts singing. Anthony sings much better with my voice than I do, but when I was transcribing the recording, something didn't seem quite right with this song, and then it dawned on me. My grandmother used to sing this, only she sang, "My eyes are blind, I cannot see." Anthony sang "I am not blind, I cannot see."

A: *They have eyes . . . I am not blind, I cannot see. I did not bring my specs with me. They have no specs . . . glasses you see . . .* (chuckle) *I love that. Love to play those games with you . . . the man and the glasses.* (Anthony started singing again.) *I am not blind, I cannot see, I did not bring my specs with me. They can't see. They can't. It's how they are. It's not your job. It's not. Your job is to see the ones that can see . . . eye to eye. Look, just look. See . . . it's so powerful. It is so powerful. Just look and see! I see you. I see you. I see you . . . feel it! Feel it. You cannot talk to them with your voice until they see you . . . until you see them.*

During the weekend event, I had several times had the urge to speak up and share but had resisted. I really wanted to speak up but was reluctant for some reason.

A: It's not a bad thing. The voice is a lower, lower quality. Oh yes, I know you want to use it. You want to say, to speak, to get it across . . . what is it? What is it you want to get across? Is there more than I see you, you see me? I am you, you are me and together we are we. Is there more? No, there is no more. This is your answer. It is the answer. I am you and you are me and together we are we. Oh yes, you can create . . . oh, you are so magnificent. You can create anything in your screenplay of life. That is really just child's play.

Here Anthony showed me a little video of my youngest granddaughter. She was drawing pictures with her crayons and telling me about them.

A: Draw it, paint it, imagine it . . . this big red squirrel, and green and this is a tree with apples. See it? There's no right way or wrong way. This is what I'm painting. That's all you need to know. This is what I am painting! I am painting my life! I choose to paint love! I choose to paint joy! I choose to paint en-thus-iasm . . . en-theos . . . with God, of God. I am of God. I am God and I am playing an Earth game, the basis of which is love. Love is the paint. Love is the paper. Love is the brush. It is all there is! Love is the creative force, the creative energy. I love. I love me. I love you. We love. It's a necklace. It's a chain. It is a band of love.

I had been in the mall across the street from the hotel the first day I arrived in Sacramento and had bought some rather expensive face cream from a young man at a booth in the center aisle. He was entertaining and a very good sales person. Later, I wondered what the heck I had been thinking. But at the time it was entertaining. I often see images of big ships when I meditate and had seen them that morning.

A: Those other things . . . the money . . . the face creams, the ships, the travel, the golf game, they are but baubles, brightly colored bits to decorate your world. A Christmas tree . . . they're ornaments. They're beautiful. They're lovely to look at, to enjoy. Create them! Make them! Have them! Love them! Enjoy them! You can you know. There is no hardship! There are no difficulties! There are no worries! There is no concern! There is only love! There is only joy! There is only en-thus-iasm . . . in God, of God, with God . . . God. There's no right! There's no wrong! There's no in! There's no out! There's no acceptable! There's no unacceptable! There's no favorite! There's no better than, less than, worse than. There is only love . . . and baubles, and things to enjoy, things you create like crafts.

Here Anthony is showing me a visual of me playing with my granddaughters, making crafts.

A: Make a pretty box . . . you stick the beads on. Oh, isn't it nice? You make the necklaces. You put the stickers on . . . like a child creating. Creating, enjoying, laughing, running, jumping, having fun, that's all there is! That's all there is! You do not need to save the world! Your job is to shine, to see them . . . to see them . . . to REALLY SEE THEM. You can

IT'S YOUR MOVIE!

look upon the ones that have no eyes, that did not bring their specs with them. Look upon them. Your light might bounce off. It might make a dent, but do not linger. Do not linger. Look upon those whose eyes can see.

Anthony started singing his little song again. And then he tells me I can see and the voice becomes quite forceful.

A: I am not blind, I cannot see, I did not bring my specs with me. You can see! You are free! CAST YOUR GAZE ON THOSE WHO SEE, SHINE IT! ROCK IT! LOVE IT! YOU ARE STRONG, POWERFUL, LOVING CREATOR GOD. ROCK IT! SHINE IT! OWN IT! STEP UP AND OWN IT! NO MORE HESITATION, NO MORE WORRYING, NO MORE CHECKING, NO MORE GAUGING OR GRADING . . . NONE OF THAT. STEP INTO IT! OWN IT! WEAR IT! YOU ARE CREATOR GOD. GO FORWARD AND CREATE!

Summary Notes:

Today, transcribing this recording, I understood something that was very powerful for me. I now know that Anthony (my higher self, my soul, the one, or the "big ME") is working with the "little me" all the time, creating an experience on this beautiful planet Earth, pointing me in the direction of joy. My higher levels present experiences and "coincidences" that tie together beautifully to give me guidance and answers and fun and experience all at the same time. An example here is the man with the glasses and the song *"I am not blind, I cannot see. I did not bring my specs with me."*

Two days prior I had been in the Phoenix airport waiting for my flight to Sacramento. An elderly couple came along and sat across from me in the waiting room at the gate. There was a gentleman sitting next to me and the four of us chatted while we waited. The elderly couple had a suitcase that was a real classic. The man next to me commented on it and the elderly gentleman told us the suitcase had been a wedding gift 60 years ago.

There were several flights leaving from the same general area at the same time and I turned my attention to the garbled loudspeaker so that we wouldn't miss our flight. I was looking away from the couple trying to concentrate on loudspeaker announcements when I thought I heard something fall to the floor. Then I heard a voice in my head say "glasses." I turned to the gentleman and asked if he had dropped his glasses. They both looked around on the floor by their bags and decided that no, they hadn't.

The elderly couple didn't hear well and the area was very congested so I suggested they stick with me until we boarded the plane. When we got on, we realized that we were seated together and we laughed about this as we settled in. Then the man started patting his shirt pocket and looking around and I knew "his glasses." He said to his wife "I think I did lose my glasses." They then explained to me that he had problems with his eyes and what he had lost were special sunglasses without which he would be would not be able to see well outside in the sun.

I stood up and swam upstream to the front of the plane where a gate agent was speaking with one of the flight attendants. When I explained the situation, the gate agent she said she would go and look for the glasses. I described the area where we had been sitting and where the glasses would be if the gentleman had dropped them there. The gate agent went looking and was able to find them quickly and bring them back.

I sense that this is not so much about learning lessons as it is about weaving a joyful fabric of life. If a voice from on high just boomed down a few words in "answer" to a prayer or question, what fun would there be in that? We could have all our questions answered in jake time and then what? Where would be the fun in that? It would be like publishing a 300 page book with 298 blank pages and 2 pages of questions and answers. I could boil this 23 minute channel recording down to this "I asked Anthony what I should do next. He said do not use your voice to try and convince those who are not ready." Instead, he wove a story, he used pictures and songs and references to other experiences. He used more than the voice. He made it fun. He concocted a beautiful creation that I could absorb and own without the need to remember.

Eleventh Channel—February 26, 2013

This was the morning of my first day back in Arizona. I watched one of Oprah's Soul Sunday videos online and then felt like I should be getting back to work on the book. I tried to organize some thoughts and themes but it just didn't seem to be flowing so I decided it was time to do another formal channel session with Anthony.

I relaxed and Anthony's energy entered my body as he prepared to use my voice. As with every time so far my eyeballs were pulled upwards. It occurred to me that this was part of Anthony's preparation to get me to "see" with a different set of eyes. I had done some reading about chakras and energy centers and wondered if Anthony was getting my physical eyes out of the way so I could see his videos and his message through my "third eye."

The total recorded time is 38 minutes. I usually do the channel session and then listen to the recording and transcribe at the same time but this day I decided to listen to the recording all the way through once before starting it over again and transcribing. I just wanted to relax and enjoy the message and I was struck again by how much of the experience is lost in the written word. I try my best to use punctuation, formatting and the odd background note to get across the fullness of the communication, but it is just not possible.

Paraphrased message:

"You do not need to save people. They are not your responsibility. You can have fun doing things, but if it feels heavy, find another way—a way that is more fun. You think you are not creative, but you are. Just because you are not knitting or painting doesn't mean you are not creating. Look up the meaning of the word *creation* and it will help you understand. You like words and you can create with them. True creation is not difficult. It flows. It comes from within and feels good.

When you are stuck in roles or identities you feel the need to protect them and you keep building layers of protection until it is difficult for you to see that you are protecting an identity. Do not think too much about what you are going to do or say and you won't have time to judge it against identities and roles you are protecting. It will just flow."

Anthony started out singing this day:

IT'S YOUR MOVIE!

A: Fly little white dove fly, way up high, way up high. Hey Tink . . . (chuckling) *you like that, don't you?*

Here Anthony is referring to my recent hypnosis regression experience with Dolores Cannon.

A: You do. It's fun. You like fun. You like happy. You like to sprinkle that fairy dust everywhere you go, and now you are free from it. You're free to do it. Free to be it. It's not a need, it's a freedom . . . sprinkle, smile, love, but you don't need to save them. No, you're just the icing, just adding to, not responsible for, just the icing . . . mmmmmm, yummy.

Anthony showed me a beautiful cupcake topped with fluffy icing and decorations.

A: Just the icing. Just have fun with it. If it feels like fun organizing, scrutinizing, wording, if it feels like fun, do it. If it feels heavy and sluggish, find another way. Do something else . . . rest, or not . . . fly, run, jump, smile, something else . . . whatever feels good. Write the script. It's the Pat movie, remember . . . write the script.

Here Anthony switches the topic and refers to my experience that morning watching Oprah's Soul Sunday video. I was impressed with how easily she communicates; she does not appear to be weighing her thoughts or deciding what to say, she just says it.

A: She's quite something, isn't she? Very creative . . . those are your words. You're all creative, that's all there is. That is all there is in that realm, in all realms. There is only creation and creation upon and by creation. It's what it is.

Hmmmm . . . Earth School . . . well, there we go with those word symbols again. School, lessons, teachers, tests, pass/fail, move on to the next grade, levels, word symbols. How else can we describe it? Yes, there's that one . . . living library. Sort of conjures up a pool of experiences and all of the books and all of the paintings and all the physical creations there to be looked at, studied, learned from, expanded upon . . . maybe, maybe that fits.

It's only creation. It's only creation. You are right. There is only one thread (Anthony was searching for words here), *only one wave, only one movement. CREATION . . . creating . . . experiencing. Yes, look that one up, get the root. It's easier that way. You're smart, you can do it. It's you anyway. I am you, you are me, and together we are we. It's helpful for you. You can feel it on the right side. You feel it. You experience it. You sense it. You hear it.*

See, the word symbols, they can't quite do it, they can't quite do it, but they're what you have, they're your tools. Make something with them. Create something with your word symbols. You've always said you weren't creative. You don't knit, you don't sew, you don't paint . . . tried that . . . it's not that you don't, you just don't want to. But at a level you crave creation.

Use your word symbols. Create a story. Create entertainment. You're witty, you can make people laugh, you can create entertainment. You do that with your verbal words. It's just another step, take it another step . . . no, it's not improv. No, and it's not retorts, which are your best modes . . . mo-dal-ities . . . (Anthony was chuckling and having a bit of fun with words) *because then you don't have to think about it. In fact, you often say, "Oh, that just slipped out," or "I can hardly wait to hear what I'm going to say," because you don't have to think about it, judge it, see how much hangs out, or consider how much trouble will this cause. Are they going to look at me funny? All those things ... it's the easiest way, isn't it? And it's fun. Create a situation, create a situation, create and experience and inter-ject fun with your words.*

Anthony was referring to improvisation or speaking without thinking it over, weighing it out.

A: *So take it to the next level* (laughing). *Move up a grade, you passed that one! You've completed improv. Now go to the next grade and experience; put it out there, experience. Here's something ... chew on this one ... does this do anything for you? "No, it's not out there for me to support or become attached to or to identify with, it's there. It's just a creation. It's a created thought or idea to expand the thinking." That's what we're doing: we're expanding the thinking. You know, expanding—now there's a word ... Some will say, "Well, that's not expansive, we heard that before, it's not new." So there expansive means new or more or better.*

I often had thoughts like these. I'd discover a new "truth" or Anthony would tell me something I thought was new ... and then I would hear someone else say the same or something similar. This had happened again watching Oprah's video that morning.

A: *Some will say "Oh, if I eat one more piece of chocolate cake, my belly's going to expand so much it won't fit my pants." There we mean expansive as growing, getting bigger ... not necessarily in a desirable way, but growing, getting bigger nevertheless.*

What does your dictionary say? Look it up. That's the auth-or-ity, you know (chuckling). *In your language, in your country, that's your authority. It supports your identity, your school, your grade, your level.*

"He has a wonderful vocabulary, ergo; he is a cut above, on a different level." It's interesting, your school game and the word symbols that support it.

Have you ever watched children playing games when they're little and haven't been corralled? When you haven't yet been able to get them to understand the rules of the game or that they need to choose an identity. The way they play ... it's total improv. That's why they love it so much. They don't think about it ... oh, is that a rule? Oh, who's turn? They only do that when you're organizing them ... turns. "Oh, no not yet, it's not your turn!" Just leave them alone and it's just improv, just improv. And as they grow older, they learn that there are rules (chuckling).

You know that book you carry around in your golf bag, The Rules Of Golf, with so many pages, so many words and printing so small you can hardly read it with glasses, with magnification ... that many rules ... to play a game, to have fun. It's no wonder it's stressful ... it's no wonder. The rules support the identities. Just put it out there ... improv ... create it, create ... create the doorway to freedom.

Here the voice was fading and searching for words. When he said the word "expiate," Anthony was having fun with it, making a rhyme. He was also reinforcing his earlier message to find another way if it was hard or not fun.

A: Create the opportunity to float, to gen-er-ate, to create, to expiate (chuckling). *Yes, that was a little bit of fun. Yes, it can't be hard. It must be easy! True creation is easy! It has no timing. It sinks down, passes through, and goes out into the field. It is a genuine want, desire, and feeling. It is impromptu. It is easy. It is ease. It feels like—heaven. It is effortless. It has no goal, no ending, no achievement no accomplishment.*

IT'S YOUR MOVIE!

It has only ease! Joyful, ease.

Then Anthony used a video of an experience I had last fall to reinforce his message. I was in Peru with about 20 other women from various parts of the world. We were sitting down to eat in a small dining room at a beautiful retreat called Willka T'ika. He retold the story to bring the images to my mind.

A: Think of that table in Peru. You're all sitting around, many Canadians, many from other parts of the world, and it's Canadian Thanksgiving Day. Your group leader says, "Let's hold hands and say something that we are grateful for to celebrate Canadian Thanksgiving." And you do. And it's lovely. And people sit there waiting their turn . . . tense a bit . . . "What will I say, will I sound stupid? Oh, somebody already said that, so I'll have to say . . . oh, you took mine." And then they get to you and you say, "I am grateful for this beautiful meal and having these loving people to share it with," and they murmur . . . mmmhummm . . . and then, without thinking (chuckle), *you say, "and I'm grateful that I didn't have to cook it," and they laugh.*

Which felt better? Of course . . . improv.

I was back to worrying about who would read this book and Anthony wanted to nip this in the bud.

A: Your book will have its own energy. Like a smile or a wink or a nod . . . a certain energy. There will be those who will be attracted. They won't know why, they won't care . . . improv.

There will be those who say to someone else, "You really should read this book," for many reasons . . . because they've been trying to get something *through to them and they think maybe if they read the book, they'll accept it . . . fixing people. And some because they enjoyed it and they want others to have the enjoyment too. No matter. No matter!*

At that point, my thoughts went to *What if no one reads it?* Anthony of course picked up on this.

*A: Oh, resistance to that, eh? . . . no matter if no one reads it. That is not why you think you're creating it. It's not how you're picturing it. You're creating it . . . you're creating a **successful** book. That's what makes it difficult, that idea that you need to create a successful book. You are creating an energy, an improv, a wisp . . . putting it out there and it, it will be. Let it come. Let it flow. Make it easy. Choose easy!*

Anthony now refers to something that happened at Dolores Cannon's weekend seminar in Sacramento. Dolores was doing group exercises with us. This one was called a little "psychological" test. She read a list of things and asked us to make note of what kind of image or thought came into our minds as she said each thing. One went something like this: "You are walking along a path and you come to a wall. What does the wall look like?" My mind sorted through several images of walls, trying to gauge which would produce the most desirable "grade." When we talked about it after the exercise, some people said they had a difficult time seeing anything.

A: You know that wall, the wall that Dolores was asking you to picture in her exercise? How many different versions flitted through your mind? How many pictures did you see? The very first one was a short wall that you could go around, and then you judged that one and came up with . . . oh . . . that great big wall. And that one quickly faded and you could go into your pretty one, that you could climb over . . . might fit best with what she was looking for . . . uhum . . . "what she was looking for" . . . making it difficult.

That's why some of those people don't see anything. They think it needs to be difficult, right, lasting, defining. They are supporting identities they can't even describe. The fanatics at least can describe their identities and support them . . . with great gusto. But those who are even afraid to put the dressings on their identity . . . they cannot do that. They cannot see. They cannot create. They are stuck. Stuck going around and around building up more and more layers like when you are making cotton candy making it harder and harder for them to see . . . to see the identity that they are protecting.

First, they need to be able to see the identity that they are protecting, for when they can see it, shine their light on it, it becomes evident, obvious to them that they no longer need, or want to (chuckle) *serve and protect that identity. They will not read your book. They, they are for someone else. They are STUCK. Do not pass go! Do not collect $200! STUCK, like a bolt stuck in place. It takes great force and great effort to loosen that bolt . . . hard knocks, hard knocks, wrenching, pounding . . . hard knocks and some never do. But they come to the place where they can no longer move at all and they are dead. They have lost the ability to move. They will not read your book.*

Summary Notes:

I was more frequently having the same experience where I would receive inspiration or messages in dreams or channels and then soon after would hear someone else saying the same "new truth." In this message I believe Anthony was intimating that there are many people disseminating what appears to be the same message. The words are similar but their energy or frequency is not and people will be attracted to the message based on their own energetic frequency at the time.

My ears always perk up when Anthony talks about judgment. It is one of the things that I would dearly like to remove from my mental repertoire. This part of the message spoke loud and clear to me:

JUDGMENT COMES FROM SUPPORTING IDENTITIES. UNTIL WE CAN UNDERSTAND AND "IDENTIFY" THE IDENTITIES WE ARE SUPPORTING, WE CANNOT FREE OURSELVES FROM JUDGMENT. NEGATIVE EMOTIONS COME FROM JUDGMENT, BOTH JUDGMENT OF OURSELVES AND JUDGMENT OF OTHERS. THIS IS HOW WE ARE INDUCED TO FOLLOW THE RULES AND TO CONFORM. JUDGMENT IS LIKE THE CATTLE PROD USED TO HERD CATTLE OR THE ELECTRIC FENCE USED TO CONTAIN ANIMALS. IT IS THE ENERGY OF CONTROL.

Twelfth Channel—February 27, 2013

I had been worrying about my children and wondering if and how I could help them with life's difficulties. I was going back and forth between minding my own business and doing something to help. I knew they needed to live their own lives and to take responsibility for themselves and was having difficulty deciding what the difference was between caretaking and caring or caregiving. I didn't want to be a caretaker but I did want to be caring. Anthony could see this tension and confusion.

IT'S YOUR MOVIE!

The channel was getting stronger and Anthony was speaking longer. This session was 57 minutes. It now consistently took between 3 and 4 minutes for Anthony to prepare my body and begin to speak.

Paraphrased message:

"Your life is like a movie and your job is to write the movie of your life. You cannot write the movie of someone else's life. You can only write your own movie describing how you would like to see it on your screen. Do not try to fix or save other people. They are creating their own lives. If it hurts to watch how other people are creating their lives, see it differently. Write a different script and let them write theirs. Your present was created by emotions, not thoughts but the emotions attached to thoughts. If you are feeling disharmony get into harmony with the feeling and you will create harmony. Get it clear what you want and it will be created by the emotions attached to the want. Be careful with the emotions for they are what create."

These are Anthony's words.

A: Calmly ... calmly now. (Anthony trying to get me to relax). *Yes, you're wound up today. Harder to break through when you're wound up. You don't see it. You can't see it on the outside. You think you're calm. You think you're relaxed because you are sitting, but you're wound up. Your head is focused. It's focused on fixing ... fixing again. "What can I do to help? Why don't they pay attention to me?" Fixing ... fixing.*

Here Anthony uses his familiar tricks of humor and videos to try and get my mind out of the way so he can talk to me.

A: (chuckle) See the pink bunny rabbit. It's bouncing along with the drum. It's the Energizer Bunny. He's not wound up. He's going with his flow. He's bouncing and drumming and smiling . . . going with, not putting any obstacles in the way, just going with, down the road past the telephone poles, drumming. Yeah . . . wide-open road ahead, straight, no bumps, no curves, just straight ahead . . . wide open. Away he goes. Away he goes. See that road straight ahead? No bumps, no curves.

Now Anthony changes to a new little video to keep me from thinking. I had recently watched the movie *Thelma and Louise* for the first time. The videos weren't working and I was still wound up, so Anthony was telling me to calm down.

A: Yeah . . . Thelma and Louise sailing down the highway, running away, they were. Calmly, calmly! Feel your foot, jiggling . . . muscles jumping in your leg . . . calmly, calmly. Breathe into it. Relax.

In addition to worrying about my children, I was wondering about the book and whether we had enough now to finish it and was worrying again about how it would be published and who would read it.

A: No, we don't have enough yet. Yes, there's more. No, don't worry about those things. Those things will come later . . . publishers, book tours all those things. Those will come later. You're on the right track, just keep moving. Just keep moving! Magneto . . . just keep moving. You're getting messages all the time now. Yes, sometimes it's cluttered . . . sometimes. Relax . . . relax . . . so many things going round and round . . . noise, white noise. Just relax.

Here Anthony uses one of his favorite themes: "It's Your Movie."

IT'S YOUR MOVIE!

A: Write the script. Watch the show. You're the star. You're the director, you're the producer, and you're writing the screenplay. Watch it. Enjoy it! When you go to the movies, you don't jump up and down and save people, you watch the show. It's what it is you know. It's what it is, one big giant theater (chuckle). *Call it a school, Earth school, the living library. It's a theater, it's a theater and you're producing the show. You're the star, you're the director, you're the producer. You write the scripts and we provide the extras, the scenes, the props . . . all of it. You just need to write it.*

It is not your job to build the props, to find the extras and the supporting actors, and train them and supervise them and feed them donuts and make sure they are happy, that their trailers are good, that everybody gets along, that they do what they're supposed to. That's not your job! That's our job. Your job is to write the movie, write the script, write the screenplay, produce, direct and star! And then watch it. Just watch it! It's the Pat show, it's the Pat show . . . easiest production there ever was. You don't actually have to be the producer or the director.

Here Anthony could sense my head getting in the way and fears starting to appear.

A: We'll do that. You just write it, write the screenplay, write the outline . . . this is what is going to happen, this is how it's going to work out, this is what I want to see . . . and then leave it to us. We'll fill in the blanks.

Here Anthony was showing me a video of me alone in a movie theater watching a movie.

A: Just sit in that seat. Put your feet up on the back of the seat in front of you. It's your theater. You can do whatever you want. Have a drink, have some snacks and enjoy it . . . just enjoy it! Feel it, hear it, smell it, sense it, enjoy it. It's your movie. It's your movie.

Anthony started singing because my mind was becoming involved again.

A: (Singing) *"The wheels on the bus go round and round. The wheels on the bus go round and round, early in the morning." It's not your deal. It's not your deal. It's their deal.* (referring to my children). *It's their deal. It hurts to watch them create what they're creating . . . "there's never enough money . . . doesn't matter, I never get ahead. I can't do it for myself, when will somebody help me?" It's not your deal. You can't change it. They can't hear you. They can't hear you. There's too much going round and round in their heads. They can't hear you. I know you want to do something and you want to know the difference between caretaking and caregiving.*

Anthony showed me a new video to help me see the difference between caretakers and caregivers.

A: You know, you see them . . . you call them caretakers. They look after the stuff that breaks, they fix it, they clean up after people, they mow the lawns and empty the trash. They're the caretakers.

You see them . . . the caregivers. They hold the hands, they wipe the tears off the cheeks, they brush the hair out of the eyes, they say, "Let's go for a walk in the sunshine." They buy a treat, they comfort, and then they go home . . . and they look after themselves. They take care of themselves.

IT'S YOUR MOVIE!

Back to my children again.

A: *They're not broken. They don't need fixing. They are creating. They are creating a movie that they don't like . . . that they don't want to watch, that it's hard for them to watch. It makes them feel bad, but it's their movie. It's their movie! You are not the caretaker. You are not the caretaker. And they are not asking. They are not asking! They are not asking for you to play a role that you can play. Write the script.*

Anthony then reminded me of something I had read somewhere:

A: *You remember what you read in a book . . . about how everybody had their own movie playing in the theater and if you went into the movie of your mother, you would see a movie that you did not relate to as being your mother? It is your mother's movie and she is seeing it the way she sees it.*

If you go into the movie theaters of your children, you will not recognize the movie you are seeing. It is the movie of their lives as they are seeing it. You cannot write their movie. You can write their parts in your movie and you can see them in your movie how you want to see them. They might not recognize themselves if they came into your theater and saw them in your movie . . . they won't. But it's your movie. Write them how you want them to be in your movie! You want them to be happy; write that. See that! Watch it play on that big beautiful screen. See it! That's all you can do. That's all you can do. That's all there is. That's all you have dominion over. Your movie, your creation, your life.

Stay in your own theater! If they come to you and ask for caregiving, see how it fits in your screenplay. "Does this fit with how I've written in my child? Does this behavior fit with how I've written out my child?" If it doesn't, you cannot go there. You cannot go there if it doesn't fit with your characters in your movie. You are not the caretaker in their theaters.

Do not watch their movies. Do not try to change their movies. Change your movie if you do not like how the scenes are playing out. Change your movie. Change your movie! Write it out ... project it ... watch it. "This is how it is. This is what I've created. I'm watching it on my screen ... my life—my life." Stay in your own theater. Stay in your own theater!

Anthony switched the topic a bit and reminded me of a scene from a few days ago. I was sitting in an airport and our flight was being called: "Passengers needing extra assistance or those traveling with small children may board now." I saw a family with two young children, one in a stroller, and watched as they hesitated and did not push forward to the front of the line. They were somewhat hidden from the view of the gate agent who was not really paying much attention. My first instinct was to rush over and "save" them and engineer the situation so they moved to the front of the lineup and the gate agent paid attention to them. But I decided it was not my job and sat back to watch how it played out.

A: It was easy in the airport, wasn't it, with those people you didn't know. You could see it then. You could see it. You had some fun with it. But, when it was your children, it wasn't so easy, was it? Got you wound up, wound up out of the flow ... going in circles, going in circles.

It's not your job. It's not your job to help them write their movies. They don't need your help writing their movies. It's not your job. Your job is to create your life ... to create what you want. Get it clear. Get it very, very clear! You know how it is. You get it clear. You have an idea and you sit down with your computer and your fingers dance. It flows. It flows out.

IT'S YOUR MOVIE!

It's done when you get it clear.

When you get the idea clear, then it's done . . . then it has happened. Get it very clear. You don't need to get it clear the entire rest of your life experience . . . not everything that's going to happen, just one thing at a time, one step at a time. Not a step like a staircase where the next step has to follow the step you just took . . . where you have to be going someplace, having a destination. One thing at a time. Get it clear. "I want . . ." and then get it clear. Get it clear.

People ask for money . . . a million dollars, five million dollars, to win the lottery . . . seems clear—seems clear, but it doesn't have the emotions, the feelings and it stops. You can't produce a movie like that. If what we get is "I want to win the lottery," there's no point starting because what comes next? It's like a stool with one leg. It can't stand. It's not enough. What comes next? Get it clear . . . with pictures, feel the emotions. It's a hard concept in your world where you work with the idea of time because it's happening all at once. It's not a progressive thing where you have "I want" and then we bring it to you.

Anthony was struggling a bit here because he was again in "there are no word symbols to describe this" territory. The concept of time is a difficult one for him to deal with because it is a 3D concept.

A: It's a simultaneous thing . . . and it isn't. It's a . . . it's a creative process (searching for words) *like that condo. It was created for you the day you got it really clear that you wanted it. But you didn't live in it for several months . . . in your time, because we needed to arrange the scenes, the other actors, and the props. We needed to guide you, to guide you to play your part because, you see that's . . . that's how it really works. You decide what you want. When you're clear, then we have begun the creation, we arrange the props and the actors and we guide you to play your part.*

The pegs, the benchmarks, the tools that we use are the feelings . . . feelings . . . the emotional signals you send out when you get it clear what you want and we create the scene to reproduce that signal. That is how when you appear to want one thing, you get what you really believe will happen. You send out the emotional signal that is attached to that want. It's not the picture or the words, it's the vibrational frequency of the emotions you feel when you say, "I want this."

Hear this! You've heard it before. Hear it! When you write, when you create that movie of you and your children, it's the emotions you project, transmit at the time you create that determine what you will see on the screen. You are creating what you will see on the screen using the vibrational frequencies of the emotions you feel at the time you create. It's like a psychological test with children . . . "Draw a picture." How they feel at the time gets painted onto the paper.

Be very, very careful with emotional vibrational transmissions, for they are creating. They are drawing your life. You have full and complete control over these emotional frequencies. You are concurrently experiencing and creating. What you created, you are experiencing and what you experience you create. It is not a jumble. It is a clarity. It is a clarity.

What you created you are experiencing, and what you are experiencing you are creating. This is how people keep creating illness. Your science tells you that your cells regenerate and then you have a new body almost every day. So how then can you perpetuate dis-ease in the body? It is only through this truth. What you created you are experiencing, and what you are experiencing you are creating. So how then do you make it change? How then does a diseased cell create a healthy cell?

I had been wondering about this. The subject of disease and healing was one I spent a lot of time thinking about.

A: It does it by changing the emotional frequency it is transmitting and this changes what it is creating. And the way to change the vibrational frequency it is transmitting is to accept the created state and get clarity on a new state. It is to accept that the transmission created the experience and to feel a different experience. It is to say, "I created disharmony by feeling unharmonious. I now choose to create harmony by feeling harmonious." It really is that simple.

Accepting that you are the transmitter allows you to change the transmission. Seeing yourself as the receiver does not allow you to change the transmission. Think of a telegraph or a radio. And you see yourself as either the transmitter who can change what is being broadcast or the receiver who is at the mercy of the transmitter. If you see yourself as the receiver, you see your possibilities for changing the transmission limited to something somebody else must do. Or you change the station hoping to get something better. Change the transmission! Take over the driver's seat... take ownership. You are the transmitter and the receiver. Change the transmission.

Summary Notes:

In this message, Anthony shone some light on illness and disease, something I had thought a lot about. He also brought some clarity for me around the whole idea of positive affirmations and goals. I had for some time been a bit uncomfortable with the idea that thoughts create, and that if you change your thoughts, you change your life. My years of studying the power of the subconscious mind and trying to use both verbal and written affirmations to direct desired outcomes—often without success—had made me question the validity of the power of "positive thinking." Anthony's explanation that it is the emotions attached to the thoughts that actually create was very enlightening for me, and one with which I felt comfortable.

CHAPTER 15:

WEEK FOUR

Thirteenth Channel—March 1, 2013

This day's session was a shorter one at 32 minutes. Anthony had begun to tackle the ideas that cause me the most consternation and the floodgates had been opened. I wanted to know how it all really works. Anthony was trying to give me as much information as I could absorb and was at the same time trying to help me to see that it is a process and that I can't see there from here.

Paraphrased message:

Anthony seemed to have spent more time trying to explain why he couldn't explain in this session than giving a clear message so what I would pass on from this message would be something like this: "Rules create entropy. They cause things to go around in circles and close off the flow. You cannot understand how all of creation works using your 3D senses. It is being revealed a little at a time as people are able to put the pieces together. The full truth cannot yet be seen."

The voice started with soft groaning and then Anthony's words as he showed me a visual of a rocket ship taking off, and then began to sing as the train came into view:

A: Blast off! Blast off. "I hear that train a comin', comin' down the track." (chuckle) *The conductor is hanging out the door with his bandana and his big smile, hat tipped back a bit on his head, waving.*

Anthony is now having fun, playing with words and chuckling.

A: There it goes, there it goes, here it comes . . . dichotomies, seeming opposites, paradoxes, paradigms (laughing) *20 cents* (chuckling), *feathers, pennies, clouds . . . all external. Comforts, like comfort food . . . hot chocolate . . . messages, messages from you to you.*

He was again referring to things I had heard and thought about, physical signs from guides and angels, things like seeing feathers and finding coins. Anthony then began to sing.

A: "I'm going to sit right down and write myself a letter and make believe it came from you. I'm gonna write words, oh sweet, they're going to knock me off my feet. A lot of kisses on the bottom, I'll be glad I got 'em" Do you see? Do you see? I'm going to sit right down and write myself a letter. I'm going to look for messages, messages that angels are watching over me. "I see it . . . see the feather 'thanks, I love you too.'" It's all you, you know. I am you and you are me and together we are we.

And then Anthony switched the topic to games and rules. Mexican Train is a domino game I had played recently.

IT'S YOUR MOVIE!

A: The game thing, like Mexican Train. What are the rules, how do we play, who wins? You have difficulty with the winning . . . and the losing. The games with rules, the schools, the systems, the boxes. It can't be . . . it just can't be. It isn't you know. It isn't.

The children, watch the children. There are no rules; there is only joy. There's running and laughing: "Oh, you hurt me, I hurt you . . . oh, let's run and laugh some more." It's only when we interject the rules . . . "NO, Tommy, it's not your turn. NO, Sally had the red bike first. You wait your turn. You just wait over here." It's only when we introduce the rules, the mores, the frameworks, the structure, it's only then that the games, the play start to be chafing, binding, and then we have those who push the rules and break the rules and so we have new rules. "How do we deal with these people who won't play by the rules? Oh, this is how we do it." And then we look at those rules and maybe they're a little too restrictive, maybe we know better now, maybe we'll change those rules a bit. Maybe we'll have a healing circle instead of a jail. That's the way the old people did it, that's how we'll do it. That's better . . . better rules. Rules . . . (chuckling) you know the lists of rules . . . see #1.

Anthony was referring to the old joke which is a list of rules where rule #1 is, "The teacher is always right," or some such thing. The only other rule is, "If the teacher is wrong, see Rule #1."

A: It just goes round and round and round when there are rules. It doesn't flow. It's not open, expansive, or fluid when there are rules. It just goes round and round and round. And eventually, like a spinning top it loses angular momentum and falls over. The rules, the rules create entropy, crashes. Systems crash. Computers crash when they get into infinite loops, when there is no movement forward or out or up or outside the rules.

So what is it really? It can't be a game. It can't be a game, that's too restrictive. Games have rules. Games have boundaries. That can't be, that's not creation. So then what is it? What is it, creative life force? What is it? What is this we are doing here? It can only be creation, expansion, creating upon creation, an infinite flow of creative energy. No resistance, no leaks, no loops. Only flow. Only flow. Like evaporation and rainfall and snowfall and rivers running to the sea . . . and evaporation? NO . . . It's not like that! IT'S NOT LIKE THAT! That is a closed system. That is not infinite creative energy. There is no more being made.

The wheels on the bus go round and round. It's not possible today to use your words to tell you what it is. It's not possible. You do not have the words. It is possible to do. It is possible to do.

Anthony is having real difficulty trying to explain creation and life purpose to me using our words. But he is going to give it another try.

A: You have a word . . . infinity. Can you grasp that? Can you grasp infinity? Can you see it in your mind's eye? You have no reference. You have no basis. Your words, your world deals in phrases like "point of reference." There is no point of reference in infinity. It is a dimensional thing and it isn't. From 2D you can see 3D and some of you can see beyond 3D . . . not with your physical eyes, not with the ones that look out and see and say, "What a pretty day," not with those eyes, with your awareness eyes, with your space eyes, with your sixth sense you can see, you can be aware.

Some of you see it very clearly. You see people who have crossed over. You see guides and angels in a physical form that you can recognize as they present themselves to you. Marshall McLuhan . . . "The medium is the message." And now you are asking for a message for which I cannot use

IT'S YOUR MOVIE!

a medium that you can recognize, and yet it is the key. It is the key. You can't be fooled with analogies of references like games or hierarchies or levels or processes. Your awareness, your awareness chokes . . . feel that (I was physically choking.) . . . chokes at those types of explanation. The closest we have come is with our words about experience and creation. We are also moving very much closer to the acknowledgment that I am you and you are me and together we are we. You see that?

Here Anthony is showing me a visual he will use again. It is a huge amount of "data" floating in space and flowing down through a funnel into an area just above a misty veil that separates the people from the "higher levels." The ideas are bits that float and collect together in the area that Anthony describes as the "picking zone."

A: You see that great, huge pool of information and it's funneled down through the veil. It's trying to push through that small opening to be released into that plane. It comes in bits and pieces and it joins up . . . they join up . . . the bits and pieces that are relevant, that go together and they form pockets, pockets of awareness. It's not yet quite into your plane. It's just there in the picking zone. Remember we talked about that before—where we put the ideas into the picking zone and they're there for anybody who wants to reach up, pick, open up, and use. It's all relevant. It's all part of the big truth. It's just fragmented—like the hard drive on your computer . . . where things get separated . . . where the information is separated and the idea may not be, is not, cannot be complete. But you can still use it. It's still usable. It is not to be discarded, it is to be used, stored, accessed, and then as more information makes its way through the bottom of the funnel and into the picking field, the field where the ideas are floating, there is one that goes with the other and another that goes with another and those who have already selected the basis of those ideas are able to pick those . . . the enhancements, the expansion.

Look at the excitement! Oh, "I knew this and now look at this, now this has been revealed and now I know this." It goes along with frequencies. It goes along with wavelengths. It goes along with like attracts like . . . magnetic. All of those beautiful, beautiful concepts that have been arranged, molded, and displayed from the ideas, the bits of information that have come through the funnel.

Yes, I know. That's just a visual. (My mind was getting involved and Anthony was responding.) *I can feel that game resistance* (chuckling). *"But there has to be a way. There has to be a way to get there from here." A little bit at a time. A little bit at a time. It grows, expands like a seed, an idea, a concept germinating, slowly growing, popping its head out of the soil finding new elements, the sun, the birds, the bees, the love and growing and reaching and expanding and feeding. It's part of it. It's creation. It's experience. Experience creates, creation experiences.*

Anthony can sense that I want more—something more concrete that my mind can grasp and understand, but there is no more today.

A: *I know you want more. I know you want more.*

Summary Notes:

I am a big-picture person and really want to see the whole picture, the entire answer, but at this point Anthony cannot give that to me using my words and my filters. This message made me go back to things he has discussed in previous messages like, "*You can't see there from here. Just keep moving, and as you keep moving, you will see farther, but you can't see here from there.*"

IT'S YOUR MOVIE!

Fourteenth Channel—March 2, 2013

I had written an idea earlier that morning and wanted to get Anthony's take on it. The idea was this: Your soul has an identifiable frequency, its name or code. You come into a body and try to raise the frequency of your body vibrations to match the frequency of your soul. When you have accomplished this, there is a clear communication channel between you and you similar to the great prophets like Jesus, Mohammed, Buddha and others who, it seems, had a clear connection to God.

And then, just as I was sitting down to start a formal channel session, a poster on Facebook happened to catch my eye. It read, "Understand that the past cannot and will not take you down. If it didn't then, it certainly can't now." I got the sentiment but found myself writing, "But it can . . . if you hang on to it. If you hang on and refuse to let go, you will not go into the future. You will not live." I did not post this comment. I just wrote it on the same piece of paper I was using for my morning question for Anthony.

As I opened the channel and Anthony prepared to use my voice, he was presenting pictures and encouraging me to relax and open up. I had become quite used to the big black steam engine and was surprised when it didn't come out of the mist toward me as it usually does. Instead, it stayed on a track running from the right side of the screen to the left, some distance away from me.

The total time on the recorder that day was 47 minutes.

Paraphrased message:

"When we use energy like the energy in coal or other types of fuel we are not generating or creating anything. We are simply directing energy that already exists. It is not your thoughts that create. It is your emotions. Emotions are blended particles of source energy. Emotions create. Positive emotions are the way you bring in more creative energy. Positive emotions raise the vibrational frequency and create more space. You can call that space potential, infinite source energy or love. Negative emotions dampen (or damp) the vibration and compress the space reducing potential for creation. A positive outlook and joyful anticipation creates space for creation and raises awareness making it easier to get answers. It is not enough to think positively. You must feel positive too. You must also keep moving forward so that you can see farther. If you stand still, if everybody stands still, that will be the end of the life experience."

These are Anthony's words. At first he is showing me things, playing with words and asking me to let go and open up. The hood was the hood of a vehicle.

A: It's a banana. It's an apple. Domineering, interfering . . . a hood. Let it go. Let it go. Open up. Open up. Let it go . . . let it go . . . let it go! It's like a revolving door, at the Bay or Eaton's . . . like a revolving door.

The Bay and Eaton's were large department stores and the ones I remember had large revolving doors at the entrance.

A: In and out, round and round like the thing on the top of that motorhome. It's an anchor. It's a fixture. It's like a turbine, you know . . . that you use to generate electricity . . . round and round, faster and faster, generating electricity, directing electricity, coalescing, funneling, directing. It's already there, the energy (chuckle). *You call it harnessing, like a horse. You put a harness on it so you can use it to do your work. You take the energy that is already there and you direct it and you call it generating. It's like a generator powered by some type of fuel. The energy is already there. It's in the fuel. You're not really generating so much as directing, so much as harnessing and directing. It's all one big revolving door, one big circle. Take the energy that's here, stored underground, dig it out and direct it. Direct it to do the things you want to do and you call that creation. That is not creation. It is not generation. It is directing. It is creating a revolving door.*

*You have a question. You have a question about your soul's frequency, your individuality in the great expansiveness of creative oneness, your code, your identification, your frequency. It's the levels thing again. It's the school, the lessons, the levels. "I've been on Earth many times and I've learned my lessons better and so therefore my soul is more evolved and has a higher frequency." How does that sit? What's the difference between that and your schools, your Earth schools? "Well, I went to a higher grade and I got better grades and so I am more **advanced** than you." Is that how you think it will work?*

I know from that perspective, from that plane, from that perspective, it seems like you need a framework, some type of system or process to relate to so that you can be comfortable, so that you can accept. And I know how difficult it must be for the mind to wrap (chuckling) *itself around a concept that has no concept, to visualize that which has never been seen with the human eye. To understand and in the understanding, to translate and transmit in your word symbols something for which there are no word symbols. It's sort of like, "You can't get there from here," and then the temptation is to say, "Well, no point in starting the journey."*

We talked about this once before, about the alley and the low light and how as you proceed, go forward, take steps and move ahead, you see farther and you see farther and you see farther. If you stand still, you will never see more than you've seen today. It will be like that revolving door, like those spinning cups. Moving, appearing to move, but going nowhere.

When you saw your train today, it did something different than what you expected. It did not come out of the mist toward you. It ran along a track and kept going. It made you a little uncomfortable; you are used to seeing that train coming out of the mist toward you, and as it gets closer you can see it more clearly and see the engineer, the conductor, and the train. Today it never got any closer. It kept moving but you, because you were not on that train, could not see it any more clearly, nor could you see where it was going.

GET ON THE TRAIN. IT'S THAT EASY. Get on the train and go! Enjoy the ride, and as you ride you will see more and more things. More potential, more actualized energies, more opportunities . . . more! Pick another piece of the idea puzzle, attach it to what you have now, go with it, play with it, show it, talk about it, introduce it, write it, of course—write it! And then get back on the train and go to the next station, the next place where you want to stop where you see another piece of the idea puzzle and fit that one in. You cannot see it from there! But that doesn't mean that what you can see is not valuable. That doesn't mean that you cannot be of assistance.

Think of the alley. If you move down the alley, you can see farther and farther and you can see potentials in doorways that might lead to opportunities, you can see doorways that might lead to dangers, you can be of assistance. You can be of service.

IT'S YOUR MOVIE!

If you stand where you are, you will only see what is visible from that location and even that will be limited by a single perspective. It may be more than those behind you can see and you may be able to shout out to them and tell them what it is you see where you are, to give them some comfort, to make them feel safe in moving to where you are. But if you all stand where you are, that will be the end. The end of the experience. The end! You know you say in business, "You're either growing or you're dying," because of that built-in need to compete, to expand, and grow in order to pay the interest on the money in your financial system.

Here Anthony is referring to things I had been learning about the nature of money and the financial system. I learned them from my friend Jacqui Dunne and from her book *Rethinking Money*.

A: The interest, that interest relates to your notion of entropy and inertia. There are many people who resist change, fear change, who want to hang out in the present and in fact would be far more comfortable going back to the past because they know exactly what happens there. Perhaps that is not a bad idea . . . what could be the harm? You wouldn't have model changes. You wouldn't know who won the Super Bowl, the Grey Cup. You would just be doing the same thing day after day knowing exactly what was going to happen. Re-creating, being on vacation, re-creating, taking a rest, knowing what was going to happen, being comfortable. Not necessarily a physical rest—it's a mental rest that's why some people can have their re-creating as a sporting activity or running or sailing. They give their mind the time off. They say, "Okay mind, you don't have to do any work for a little while because we are not going to make anything new, we're just going to re-create, we're not going to worry, we're not going to experience anything other than what we feel comfortable with." And why is that? Because we've given our mind the time off. We've allowed ourselves, we allow ourselves . . . we allow ourselves

Here there was coughing and Anthony was searching for words.

A: *We allow ourselves to give our mind the time off. Because at some level, we know that it is our mind that is actively creating new experiences and old experiences and the same experiences.*

This was definitely odd. I was coughing and it was difficult to talk—and the voice had switched to first person. Perhaps my mind was interfering with the channel. This lasted only a short time and then the voice grew strong and switched back to third person.

A: *It is our mind.* (stronger voice now) *It is really your mind that is keeping you stuck in the same experiences, experiences that no longer serve you. If you're in a, say a work situation where you love the work, do you look forward to a vacation? Do you crave and need recreation? No. You are doing the work you love. There is no need. There is no need, so is it really your mind that's creating the "stuckness" that is re-presenting an experience that you judge as bad or unlikable? Is it really your mind?*

Your mind is your toolbox. Your mind helps you calculate time and distance, size and weight, all those things if you need to do your job, play your games, look after children, build things, fix things. All those things. So is it really the thoughts that you think that go out and bounce back and re-create, re-present experiences that you don't feel comfortable with, that you don't like that you are frightened of? Is it really your thoughts? It's your emotions. IT IS YOUR EMOTIONS!

Thoughts are things. They are waves . . . THEY GO OUT BUT THEN THEY GO AROUND. They transform. It's like you taking the coal out of the ground and generating electricity, re-directing, harnessing, re-presenting. It's like the revolving door. Thoughts . . . so in that way they do go out and come back, not necessarily in the same way.

Emotions, now there's a different story. Emotions are blended... blended particles of source energy. They are... THEY ARE THE PATHWAY TO EXPERIENCE. Emotions create! Emotions create experiences and experiences create emotions. Emotions therefore are blended source energy. It is a focus... a focus of source energy. It is source energy focusing source energy. There isn't a... there is not a... (Anthony was searching for words) *framework, a physical plane framework to describe that because the only type of creation for which there are frameworks and terminology on the physical plane are the type that is re-directing. It is re-directing energy. It is not creating, it is not generating. It is re-directing. "I take those materials, I make paint, I paint a picture, I have created a piece of art. I re-directed the energy."*

Emotions, emotions, in order to create emotions you must pull in energy from source. It is also a re-direction of energy but it is a re-direction of infinite source energy. Emotion is the way in which the physical plane brings in more energy. Emotion is the way in which energy is expanded in that plane. There are not exactly boundaries, but there are... and not limits. There again there are not words, no word symbols.

To ease your mind, think of it in these terms... emotion is a creative way to add energy to a plane. There is that possibility, but not all emotion attracts and uses energy from the infinite source. Those emotions you label negative do not attract energy from the infinite source. Those emotions you label positive do. Negative emotions dampen energy. Negative thoughts, just as positive thoughts, re-direct energy. Negative emotions dampen energy. Positive emotions attract energy. It is not an expansion. It is an attraction and a heightening, a... a... (Anthony was searching for words again) *vibrational change. It is in that way expansive because to increase vibrational frequency increases the space between the* (searching) *the atoms . . . the particles and therefore increases the potential.*

Potential is love. The potential is the source. It's how it works. It's how . . . it's how you attract more infinite source energy which is love through positive emotion. You raise the vibrational frequency and it vibrates faster, there is more space, potential, infinite source energy, love, available. Negative emotions dampen that.

Just as with cotton candy or soapsuds, if you keep spinning, you increase the space between the sugar or the soap. If you put water on it, it compresses. The space is no longer there as potential to create the cotton candy or the bubble.

Get on the train. Enjoy the ride. Anticipate. Joyful anticipation! Joyful anticipation will bring the train quickly to the next station, the station with the next piece of the puzzle, the next part of the idea, the next attractive bit. Positive emotions create space for love.

Summary Notes:

The last few channels were more difficult to get into. I believe it was because I desperately wanted answers. I wanted to be able to describe in words and see in pictures that which cannot be told in words or shown in pictures. I thought if I could get my mind out of the way, these messages would flow more easily and more quickly and so I tried harder to quiet my mind and let Anthony come in more fully. What Anthony was telling me was to stop trying hard, relax, and get into a state of joy; this would open up the potential for creative expansion, allowing me to see higher and further.

Fifteenth Channel—March 4, 2013

In the night I had experienced either a vision or a vivid dream. In this vision/dream, I saw a small bit of sand and then I felt my arms tingling and vibrating rather strongly. I was a bit alarmed at first and then somehow I understood that my arms were being eroded and I was being changed so that I could form part of the sand. The sand then appeared as little trails or pathways through some vegetation.

I wrote this dream experience in my journal as soon as I got up so that I would remember it, and as I did this I recalled thinking in the night that I should write it down then because it felt important. But I drifted off instead and woke up again with a vague feeling of another dream, one that I couldn't quite remember. Anxiety started to creep in until I heard, *"Do not worry. You will remember what you need. If there was an important message in that dream, it will come again."* When I was fully awake in the morning, the only thing I remembered was the sand dream and it was still very vivid.

That morning, before sitting down to do this formal channel session, I had watched a YouTube video of a guy painting a picture. He was painting very quickly and it just seemed to be flowing out of his brush. A few days earlier I had seen a video of a different painter who was doing something that might be called automatic painting. He did not have a preconceived image of what the painting would look like when he was finished. These are the YouTube videos Anthony referred to in this message. I don't even remember how I came to see these videos. It just seems that links show up in emails or on Facebook and my fingers do the walking.

This was again a shorter recoding—24 minutes. Talking started at three minutes. During that time Anthony talked to me, telling me that I needed to clear out the space for him, to let go. He also showed me some vivid images. My mind was a big room inside my head that and it was being swept out until it was empty and sparkly clean. Then a beautiful column of blue light entered my head through the crown and flooded my body. These were not images I was consciously trying to create in my mind. They were images Anthony was displaying for me. The voice today was also stronger and deeper. I have come to recognize this tone as Anthony with "me" out of the way.

Paraphrased message

You do not create with your conscious mind. Creation flows through you. If you just approve of what is happening, do not judge, and release expectations and attachments to outcomes, you can be in joyful anticipation all the time. You are not an Earth toy being guided on a predetermined plan by guides on a higher plane. We are really YOU and our messages are you talking to you. The bigger YOU is creating the experiences for you. You have already approved the experiences being created.

These are Anthony's words.

A: Are we clear? Are we clear? It is my message today. No questions! No worries! No butting in! It is my message today. My message to you and you and you, everyone. Hear this today. Today . . . is the first day of rest

IT'S YOUR MOVIE!

of your life . . . good one.

Anthony could feel my mind butting in and used a bit of humor and then a stern reminder to get me out of the way.

A: I asked you to get out of the way, to let me be the messenger. Be the receiver! Open it up, clear it out, be the receiver! Yes, that was us in the night; we were upgrading, fixing, working. Accept it. Let go! Let go, you're doing fairly well on the body image thing. Do you see how much easier it is when you don't try, when you just notice? Makes you feel good doesn't it? Like in Sacramento when you went to use that public washroom and after you left you noticed that you hadn't looked in the mirror, you hadn't checked yourself over, you hadn't assessed, judged. You didn't even look. You didn't try. Trying isn't the same . . . processes, working it out step by step. That's not where it is. Where it is, is in noticing. Noticing is an experience. Experiences create. Creation experiences

When you notice, you're noticing something that you did not consciously create. You cannot create consciously.

That YouTube video this morning . . . did you like it? He was just letting it flow, seeing it in his mind's eye, perhaps, and letting it flow. Just letting it flow. He was the instrument, his body, the paints, the canvas. He was painting what he was creating. Not step by step. Not take a photo, sit down at an easel, make an outline, start to fill it in, whoops, cover it up. That was the second of the painting things we showed you, wasn't it? The other one didn't know what he was going to end up with. He just started and if it didn't feel right, he painted it over with white and started again. Something like those puzzles your son does where he doesn't know what the picture is going to be—he just starts making the puzzle.

Anthony is referring to the jigsaw puzzles my son puts together where either the puzzle does not look like the picture on the box or there is no picture on the box.

A: Much easier, much more enjoyable, less judgment, less fear, fun. We told you we could fix your body and all we needed was your approval . . . (chuckling) you remember? We weren't asking for you to approve us fixing it. We were asking for you to approve, to detach.

Yes, you're going for a haircut again today, and you've decided to trust the stylist . . . to just let the stylist cut your hair, to approve in advance. Ah, look at that, that means you can feel good before you even do it . . . interesting. That means you can have joyful anticipation, knowing that it's all going to work out and that, in all likelihood, it will be better than you could have imagined. That's what we are asking for—approval. Let us do it in our way with our result and know that it can be better than you could imagine.

Joyful anticipation. If you do that with everything, if you just approve . . . just approve, then you can be in a state of joyful anticipation all the time. Not expectation, expectation has attachments. Expectation causes tightness. Expectation does not allow for better than you could possibly have imagined . . . like your friend Jennifer says, the "or better."

When he says Jennifer, Anthony is referring to Jennifer Hough who, although she does not want to be guruized (her word), has been a great mentor and friend to me.

A: Expectation allows for failure, or perceived failure, judgment, resentments, all those things. Approval, prior approval, allows for joyful anticipation. Relaxed, calm, happy. I told you before you do not need outside approval. You are pre-approved. There is no expectation of you. There is no plan, no group of spirit people gathering around conferencing on how well you're doing with the plan. "Oh, she's not doing what we expect so we'd better do something here." No, there isn't. You are pre-approved. You are stronger than that! You are bigger than that! You are much more powerful than that!

You are not a little rat we put in a maze to watch how you run around and get through it. NO. You are you and I am you and together we are we. You saw that, didn't you, when you were reviewing your transcriptions and you thought perhaps you had mistyped or mis-heard. No, you didn't. I meant exactly that. You are you and I am you and together we are creators, crea-tor, crea-tion. You are not a toy. You are not a hope or a wish that was sent out from on high to perform some magic on a plane that was taking a nose dive. NO. That is not what you are! You are magnificent creation. You are pre-approved! Can you see it? Can you see it?

Here Anthony was showing me a visual of a thin, wispy cloud-like veil floating in the air.

A: The thinning of the veil. Can you see how big you are? Feel it! Absorb it! You have a hand in it. You are not a toy! You are not a project, an experiment, a wishful thinker, a hope, the last hope for Earth—that is not what you are. None of you! You are all pre-approved! Warriors with nothing to fight, only the strength to bind together to create something so powerful, so impressive, so magnificent that it explodes in gratitude. That it produces, that it magnifies, that it expands, that it intensifies, that it envelops and unfolds... all those words and none of those words... there are no words. Just know, just know... YOU ARE PRE-APPROVED.

During this little "speech," Anthony showed me a visual of a beautiful shower of sparkling stars and then a big bolt of lightning. He was on a roll.

A: There is no need to fix or guide or prod or poke. Our communication, our messages are you talking to you. They do not come from us to you to guide you in the way that a dog trained to do so will guide a person with limited physical sight. No.

Do you see that lightning? Do you see that lightning bolt? It is something like that . . . where the charge, the seeking, is built up from both sides until at once it comes together and forms a beautiful light. You have those expressions, "Oh, she finally saw the light," "Oh, the light came on," ideas . . . you use images of light bulbs to represent them. It's the closest I can come today. It's the closest we can come today. Your puppy dogs, your kitty cats . . . I see it. Another day. Another day.

Summary Notes:

The experience with the washroom and the mirror came during the weekend I went to Dolores Cannon and Dee Wallace's event. We were given a 10 minute bathroom break and since there were close to 60 women in the group, the line-up at the women's washroom located near the seminar room was long. I really needed to go so I ran up the stairs and found another washroom. As I was going back down the stairs, it dawned on me: *You didn't look in the mirror; you didn't check yourself out.* This was definitely a new experience. If you have ever been in a women's public washroom, you will know what I mean. Some are quite open about it, looking and peering, combing and fixing. Some even spread out a makeup kit and do some real work. Others might just take a peek when they are washing their hands or look back over their shoulders as they leave the sink. In my experience, it is rare for anyone to not even look. But that day I didn't. I remember saying to myself, *Oh, you must have looked, you just can't remember what you saw.* And then I heard, *No, you didn't look.* This made such an impression on me that it was one of the notes I wrote in my journal that night.

The whole body image thing has been a real deal for me. For years, I wouldn't be caught dead outside of the house without having showered, done my hair, and put on makeup. These were the first things I did in the morning. Gradually, over the years, I allowed myself to go out for a walk or run to the store without makeup. And then, rebel of all rebels, I went one day without a shower. This was big!

My body has produced a variety of aches and pains and illnesses throughout this lifetime, and at one stage about 20 years ago, I was getting a massage every week to try and ease the pains in my neck, back, and arms. I remember quite clearly the massage therapist telling me how much he liked the weekends because he didn't have to bathe if he didn't want to. My immediate thought was, *Why would you not want to . . . how could you be comfortable not having bathed?* It is a point of hilarity in my family when my daughter, who at 37 is a size two, and myself, who at 62 is a size six, start complaining about our fat arms, flabby bellies and jiggly butts. We notice we are attached to a body image and judge ourselves accordingly. So for me to not even have a little peek check in that bathroom mirror was almost monumental and it certainly made me sit up and take notice.

And today I am getting a haircut. This is another major piece of the body image puzzle. My husband was accustomed to me fuming through the door after another hair salon experience. I would march in and head straight for the bathroom where I would wash my hair and re-do it. It became a family joke: "It will look fine once you wash it yourself." There have been only a few exceptions to this "getting my hair done" process. A couple of years ago, I went to visit a friend in California. My hair really needed "something" and my friend made an appointment for me with her stylist. There was something different about him; he seemed to be looking at me like a lump of clay thinking, *What can I make with this?* and for some reason, I didn't feel the need to give instruction. I loved the cut. It was different and I didn't even consider rushing home to wash and restyle.

Anthony had given me a little message a few days ago when I was standing looking in the bathroom mirror, bemoaning the fact that my hair was falling out and generally looking scraggly. I heard a gentle voice in my head: *Remember that hair cut you got in Palm Springs, how effortless and fun it was? Just do that.* So today, that is what I plan to do. My hair cut is pre-approved.

Last night I was reading through transcriptions of the messages I had channeled so far and the notes and drafts I had already written. Although I had listened to each channeled message at least twice and had transcribed the messages myself, I was absorbed in the reading. Images were displaying, experiences that had made impressions throughout this life and were somehow stored in my subconscious were woven together, intermingling with Anthony's messages and my notes, calming me, soothing me and weaving a beautiful tapestry of happy emotions. It is not possible to describe the feelings, the depth of my appreciation, or wonder as I "watch" the coming together of what I think of as memory movies, remembrances that join together to deepen and unfold. I can only hope that somehow,

IT'S YOUR MOVIE!

through my sharing and through Anthony's messages, you can add to or trigger your own memory movies and create the same delicious feelings in yourself.

That morning, after writing in my journal, getting my coffee and settling myself in my big comfy chair, I checked emails and then moved on to Facebook. One of my friends had posted a link to a YouTube video of a contestant on one of the talent shows on TV. The contestant said he was a speed painter and that he would do a painting in a minute and a half or less. He was busy painting and the panel was busy trying to figure out if they could see anything recognizable on the canvas. The moderator was announcing the time. "You have one minute left . . . 30 seconds now . . . coming down to the wire . . . 15 seconds." The painting still looked like some paint splashed randomly on a canvas. At one second, the contestant turned the picture "upside down" and it was a beautiful picture of a gentleman in profile. The panel was floored and amazed. So was I.

The other painter Anthony referred to was also someone I had seen on the Internet. I didn't watch that entire video, just enough to get the gist. The young man didn't know what the painting was going to look like. He just started in one quadrant of the canvas and painted. If it didn't look right to him, he painted over it with white and started again. When he had completed the quadrants, the picture took shape.

This story had my mind wandering back to images of one of my friends telling a joke at a Rotary Club meeting. He was actually doing a "this is my life" presentation, something we did in the club to help people get to know each other better. This gentleman was a retired city police chief who had taken up wood carving in his retirement. Mostly he carved ducks and he said it was very easy because all he had to do was cut away anything that wasn't a duck. Sort of Michaelango-ish.

My son has always loved puzzles. As a very young child, he would put together puzzles with hundreds of small, similar-looking pieces. Later, when 3D puzzles became available, we bought him one of those, and now his wife buys him puzzles where either the puzzle looks different from the picture shown on the box or there is no picture on the box. His daughter is also a puzzle aficionado. We had a drawer full of puzzles in the living room each with over a hundred pieces. Our granddaughter has now moved on to computer games but at two or three years old when she would visit, the boxes would all be pulled out and she would have them laid out on the floor, all put together before we could even say "relax." Often she would say, "Nana, sit on the floor and help me." I would oblige and in my adult "I know better" mode would try to "help" her.

When I did puzzles as a child, I stood the box on its side and looked the picture over carefully so I would know what I was "making." After I had the picture in my mind, I found the outside pieces and put them together so I would know how big the project was and could monitor my progress. After the outside, I sorted the pieces by color to match the picture on the box. When I tried to help my granddaughter by teaching her this system (which was of course how it should be done) she just batted the box away and put the puzzle together. Gradually I figured out that she was doing it by shape. She saw by their shape which pieces fit and put them together. Go figure.

"You are you and I am you and together we are we." When I was reading through the transcriptions last night, I saw this in channeled message

four. Still, after almost a month of channeling and everything I have seen and experienced in the process, I sometimes wonder if this is all just something I am doing at some ego level. So when I saw these words instead of the ones I had become so accustomed to *"I am you and you are me and together we are we."* I got a little anxious. Had I heard it wrong? Did I type it wrong? Was something wrong? Anthony picked up on that worry.

I am beginning to get a sense of the peace that is available if we just accept what is happening, go with the flow, piece the memory bits together, and watch the puzzle take shape.

Anthony's last words, *"Your puppy dogs, your kitty cats . . . I see it . . . another day, another day"* are in response to musings and questions I had that morning around illness in pets. I was seeing more pets with tumors or diabetes or some form of disease. I wanted to have an answer to how and why this was happening. My whispering instincts were telling me that we have brought these animals so close to us that they are operating in our wavelengths or frequencies and our pets may in some way be "taking one for the team" by manifesting illnesses created by the emotional signals of their owners. I will just leave that one for now, knowing that the answer will be revealed when and if the time is right.

Sixteenth Channel—March 6, 2013

The night before this channel session had been a restless one for me. In my dreams I had been shown a series of what I can only describe as "visuals." They were not really images or things I could see clearly. It was more like a different type of seeing with different planes or dimensions. While I was dreaming, it all seemed quite clear to me, but when I awoke, it was not.

The total time for today's recording is 37 minutes. As I relaxed, my mouth started moving and my eyeballs were being drawn up while my eyelids were being drawn down. There was some soft moaning and very softly the words *"Mexican train"* (I was seeing the train visual), and then after 2 minutes Anthony started talking.

Paraphrased message:

Today Anthony talked again about words and how we are comforted by our words and the meanings we attach to them. The message is, "Although your reasoning mind is comforted by words and is most comfortable when you can put your thoughts into words, truth is something you sense or feel, not something you try to learn or understand. Words are part of the fun, the physical experience. Truth just is and you can feel it. Words are colored or changed and take on different meanings depending upon your physical experiences, filters, and ways of looking at the world."

Here are Anthony's words.

A: (Very soft) *Hello* (then stronger), *Good morning. Help, that's a funny one... how your computer changes your words.*

I had been talking with a friend about how our phones and tablets change what we think we are typing into different words . . . autocorrecting or helping, which in some cases is funny. I mentioned that I send my granddaughters, whom I fondly refer to as my dollies, emails every morning and that my tablet often changes *hello* into *help*.

A: Words, labels, stamps, designs, outlines, comfort . . . comfort for the mind is your words. Umhmm . . . "I can understand it because I can say it in my words." You don't need to understand it. You only need to feel it. Let feelings be your new words. Keep using your word symbols . . . chitter, chatter with your friends and family, but don't get attached to them. You don't need them . . . like your hummingbird and your friend's question, "How do you know it's the same bird?" You just know, you can feel it, you can sense it, you can see it to a certain extent but you could sense it when he was flying up behind you. You didn't need to see his pretty purple neck feathers to identify him. You could sense him, feel it. You didn't need a picture to compare with, you just knew. That's how it is, that's how it is!

Anthony was referring to a conversation I had recently with a friend about the hummingbird I call Humphrey who adopted me, and the feeder I hung in our yard in Arizona. I had been visiting with neighbors across the street a few days before. We were sitting in their back yard and Humphrey did a fly by. I sensed him coming up behind me. He flew by quite close to my head and then stopped several yards in front of me where he performed a little air dance and then whizzed away. I told this story to another friend and she looked at me a bit quizzically and said "How do you know it's the same bird?" I just knew.

A: You can feel the energy of it . . . like those puppy dogs; they can feel the energy of it, the oneness, the connectedness, the love. They don't wait for you to talk. They don't wait for you to say "Come here, come." . . . No, they don't.

I often have experiences with dogs where they seem to be communicating with me. One day a woman was walking her dog on a leash in our neighborhood. I was walking about two blocks behind them and the dog stopped and sat down. The woman turned to look back at the dog and it turned to look back at me. She urged her dog to continue but it just sat there. And then the dog turned itself around completely so that it was facing me and sat until I got there to pet and speak to it. It then happily continued on with its owner.

A: Just like the day you were leaving to go home at Christmas time and the hummingbird flew to the front and sat on the bush and watched ... an unusual thing in your mind. You only talked to him in the back yard ... with your words ... but there he was.

Words can be happy things, expressing your joyful feelings. Words are expressions, they help to express the way you feel. In that way, they can connect ... but you know that it isn't the words that tell most of the story. No, it's the feeling. The feelings show, they show in all kinds of ways, in body language, in smell, and in energy. You can feel it. You can feel it! Some of you can see it. Some of you see it in colors and shapes, filtered through your own right and wrongness. This color means this and that color means that.

There are colors, of course. You see them. They are light filtered through a medium, displayed separately ... but not. They're beautiful and they can be put back together into the magnificence of pure light which has no color and cannot be described using word symbols or comparisons. It can only be felt or sensed or perceived or none of that.

Here Anthony showed me a little video of a mountain stream.

IT'S YOUR MOVIE!

A: Yes, you see that stream trickling down the mountain bubbling over the rocks . . . you see it? What color is it? The color of movement? The color of reflection? The color of bits and organisms moving with it? What color is it? What color is glass? The sands that have been heated . . . what color is it? What color is the veil, the filters between dimensions . . . what color is it? Change the filter, change the color . . . like the settings on your TV . . . sports, normal, cinematic. What color is it? What color is it? When you look through the glass, can you see the glass? You can see the bits of dust and dirt and rain drops and reflections and coatings. Can you see the glass? It's something like that.

The dimensions, you call them 3D, 5D, 6D. It's something like that. You can't see them. You can't see the panel between that separates . . . and not . . . what you call dimensions. You can only feel it, sense it, receive it. There's not one word that can do it. Intuition, intuit . . . that's helpful . . . until it attracts dust or a film or water spots like the glass in your car windows and becomes less useful, less easy as it becomes more noticeable.

That's what happens with your word symbols, they take on attachments and bits and pieces that change their usefulness, their suitability for the purpose. That's one of the things that makes word symbols improbable . . . or unsuitable, or impossible to use to describe that which you cannot see with what you call the naked eye. It becomes a joyful test (chuckling) *then, does it not . . . to receive and then to transmit using word symbols.*

I believe Anthony is referring to the test he has in trying to guide me using words and also the test I have in trying to understand our channeling experience, which contains much more than words, into words in a book.

A: You must weave your way through all the attachments and bits and pieces stuck to those words... use enough different ones or find ones that those for whom the message is meant can comprehend best. That's all it is. No right word, wrong word... only the most attractive word, the most appealing word (chuckling again) *... the word with the best fit.*

Yes, it's something like that (chuckling) *if the wind blows, they twirl and become something different, show something different, movement... something like that. It's a process. It's a process... the upgrading. It's a process of joy. Just as you search for words to get your meaning across to your readers, we search for ways to show you more. Different ways for different people. You don't all like the same movies, you don't all read the same books, watch the same TV shows, or like the same houses* (chuckling) *... or luggage.*

I had been wanting new luggage and had recently spent time on Amazon searching and reading reviews of different brands.

A: *Try to strip the meaning, the attachments, the bits and pieces and raindrops from the words. Try to feel them, feel the word... envelop the word.*

This is the second time Anthony used the word *envelop*. Perhaps he was playing with me?

A: *Intuit the word, hear it, see it, smell it, feel it. Feel it. We will help you with the word symbols. Accept them, receive them, and use them. They have power. They have a power you cannot see. It is beyond what you call energy. It is a power you cannot see. You can only feel... feel.*

It is possible you know to strip words of attachment, of clinging bits, and pieces (young people changing the vocabulary) *... it is possible,* *through combinations and emotions transmitted with the words.*

You know about the one they call Emoto who transforms water using words. It is he who transforms the water with the emotions he transmits with the words. (Funny that his name is Emoto.)

A very powerful word in your word symbol bag of tricks is Love. It does not mean the same thing to all, and meaning has to do with how the words are received, processed, and transmitted. Words in that way have power. Words are symbols just as sacred geometry, numbers, pictographs, and shapes. All those things have power based on how the symbol was transmitted, and received. It is the emotion attached to the word as it is transmitted that imparts the power.

Words can be cleaned just as windows are cleaned. Words can be cleaned. (Laughing) *If you say that dirty word, we'll wash your mouth out with soap. A clear, joyful transmission cleans the word. The receiving can either further clean, muddy, or simply channel the word to be transmitted again.*

Words are like the revolving door, like the spinning cups, like the windmill. They go round and round and round . . . collecting, transforming, changing . . . beacon . . . attracting, warning . . . word symbols. They are one of God's creations as powerful as e-lec-tricity. (chuckle)

(Singing) *I see that train a comin', comin' down the track. We will give you more unseen, unspoken guidance that will help you with this message* (dreams). *It might disrupt your sleep to a certain extent. We'll try and keep it flowing slowly enough that it doesn't do that.*

I had very little sleep the night before.

It is important for you to ... no ... it is part of your gift, part of your piece of the puzzle ... the ability to use words in a way that does not, cannot be described with words, where it cannot be patented or claimed or written in a scientific paper, where it can be so helpful, so mighty that it is beyond, beyond, beyond.

Summary Notes:

I had heard and even believed that if you understood something well enough, you could put it into easily understandable words for others. This quote attributed to Einstein comes to mind: "If you can't explain it simply, you don't understand it well enough." Before Anthony, I had bought into this concept quite heavily. Today, Anthony showed me that understanding is (as Jennifer Hough would say) "the booby prize." Understanding is a 3D conscious mind concept and by trying to "understand" we limit our ability to sense that which we cannot put into words, for which, in fact, there are no words.

Words have intrigued me for a long time and I have often thought about the evolution of our language, how generations change the meaning of words, and how words come into popular use and end up in the dictionary. Young people now call things they admire "sick" and where we were once "up for something" they are now "down" for it. Words are a fascinating part of the human experience, and they can also be a trap.

Parents and other oldsters lament the way the younger generation prefers to text rather than speak, and I was recently made aware that "society" is concerned because the kids in elementary school can't read handwriting.

IT'S YOUR MOVIE!

Words are very tied up in the right and wrong of things. There are right words to use when you speak to your elders, pray to your Gods, and try to make a sale. There are words that praise and words that berate. The spoken word is enhanced by things like nuance, tone, and volume. Even so, many spoken words are misunderstood because they are heard through the filter of the listener. Written words are even trickier because most people "hear" words when they read. The trouble is, they hear these words solely through their own filter and therein lies the trap.

Words can be fun and they can add enjoyment to our life experience. And just like many other processes and systems created by and for humans, they can also be a trap. We are taught to play "the game of words" at a very young age and words are woven into the fabric of the roles and identities we assume and protect. It starts when we are babies with the introduction of good and bad. We learn very quickly how good little boys and girls act and what happens when we are bad. When we go to school we quickly learn about right and wrong. This is very powerful conditioning and it is easy for our egos to keep us caught up in the judgment and defensive actions that have been built around the use of word symbols as our primary method of communication.

I was once taught that only about 20% of communication comes from the words we say and the rest comes from body language. Maybe so, but I think what we are doing is translating body language into words. We are "hearing" another's body language. It still boils down to words and how we interpret them based on our own life experience and filters.

Anthony was telling me that the need to make myself comfortable by putting everything into word symbols so I could understand dampens my vibratory frequency and limits my ability move forward.

So is there really a problem with texting instead of speaking? Young people have created a new shorthand language for texting. Perhaps they are also using more intuition in their communication. Perhaps the systems around word symbols are becoming less confining . . . who really knows?

CHAPTER 16:

WEEK FIVE

Seventeenth Channel—March 13, 2013

I had been doing Oprah and Deepak's guided meditations every morning and it was becoming easier to connect with Anthony. My usual process was to set the intention to channel, get into a comfortable physical place, and then do some relaxation and breathing exercises while Anthony appeared and prepared the channel. That morning Anthony appeared quickly. As soon as I sat down, he was showing me the train and I was hearing, "I hear that train a comin'." For the first two minutes, Anthony showed me a little video of me floating on a lily pad. At the same time, my body was experiencing physical sensations. There were energy buzzes moving through, my muscles were twitching, and I was watching myself floating on a lily pad and relaxing. And then Anthony started to talk. The recording was 25 minutes long.

PATRICIA McHUGH

Paraphrased message:

Your life experience is like a movie. Write the script and then sit back and enjoy the show. Do not be concerned about details and controlling. When you do this, you give control of the script to others. Write the script and then let go of controlling how it plays out. Give up expectations and attachments to "how." Watch it unfold without resistance. Be the example of joyful experience. Do not try to teach with words; be the example.

These are Anthony's words:

A: Hand over the microphone. Sit on the lily pad. Look at the bees, float, check the clouds. What do they look like? Oh, there's an elephant. Just float . . . just float. Let it go. Let it go!

Anthony then changed to a new visual, leading me away from conscious thought.

A: Umhum . . . It's a coal chute, a coal bin—dusty, dirty, black coal . . . stinky. Umhum . . . useful on your steam engine, but you don't really want to touch it or see it.

Although Anthony came quickly and easily this morning, he still had to work to get my head out of the way. He introduced one little vignette after another.

A: No, no, just sit and look out the window. Don't think about that. Just look out the window . . . (chuckling) Yes, yes, there are Indians riding horses alongside the . . . well actually, they're riding away. Umhum . . . just sit. Look out the window. Watch the world go by. Enjoy the sound

IT'S YOUR MOVIE!

of the wheels on the tracks, the gentle rocking motion. Close your eyes if you'd like, take a little nap. You won't miss anything. There'll be a big loud announcement before anything happens. Something like your alarm clock on those days when you want to get up at a particular time. . . "You don't want to miss nothin'."

Anthony could sense me relaxing and he was having a bit of fun.

A: *Just turn it off, go to sleep, have a nap. Step out of the way. Umhum . . . Let the world go by. Let the world go by, spinning, rotating, doing its thing. Just let it go. Digging your heels in won't change it. Running from here to there doesn't change it.*

Anthony was referring to my anxiety on the golf course that week when I had played with people who were slow. The course marshal was buzzing around indicating we needed to speed up, and instead of keeping my mind on my own game, I was trying to get my playing partners to speed up without being overly rude. As a consequence, my game deteriorated.

A: *Trying to move them along, shuffle them along, hurry them up only changes you and the results you get . . . not so much results, the experience you have, the emotions you create. You forget—you forget that they're bit players in your movie. You forget to write them the way you want them. You let them take over the screenplay. They aren't even aware, they don't even want to. You just hand it to them.*

Here Anthony showed me a new visual. I was driving a car.

A: *It's like letting go of the wheel and jumping out of the car. All you get are bumps and bruises. It's your life. It's your movie! You can write it the way you want it. But you can't do that when you take your eyes off the road, your hands off the wheel, and start handing out pens to all the bit actors, all the stuff, all the props, all the extras. It's about control and it isn't. It's about keeping the control. It's about staying in charge, not giving up control. It's about staying in charge, writing the screenplay the way you want to see it. YOU KEEP THE PEN. You write it! Do you want to see a bed that's made rather than one that's unmade? If that's what you want, write it that way. JUST DON'T WORRY ABOUT HOW IT GETS DONE. Just write in the screenplay: The bed is made— period. You don't need to write notes for supporting props. You don't need to say, "This is why the bed is made or how the bed is made or any of those things." Just write: The bed is made. The same with the dishwasher. Just write: The dishwasher is loaded. And then leave it. Know that it is done.*

Undo the attachments. It's the attachments that cause the worry, the angst. It's the attachments that cause the resistance. It's the resistance that lowers the energy, which causes the emotions that bounce back and provide experiences that are not what you want or think you want.

Here we moved to a new visual. My digestive system was sluggish and I had been visualizing my food being digested in a happy stomach and then the parts my body didn't need being flushed through intestines made of shiny stainless steel.

A: Yes, that shiny stainless steel drum. Keep it clean. Let them just swirl around and down and gone. You don't need to know where they go. It doesn't matter where they go. They come in the top and just swirl around happily and they're gone. Nothing to it. They can't stick. It's slippery and shiny and sparkly and happy . . . nothing sticks. Nothing sticks. Nothing causes anything else to build up, back up, or blow up. It just all slides right down. Yes, it can be that easy. Yes it can.

Do the things you like. Notice things. If they grab your attention, pay attention. Enjoy things, do things. Be the example, not the creator of systems or structures or "shoulds" or "musts" or "If you do this then it will be okay," or "If you do that then this will happen," or "Oh, no, what's going to happen here?" Just be the example. Be the example of joyful existence. Be the example of creation creating a joyful experience.

You know how cells replicate . . . there's one and then it divides into two. Be the one that you would like to see replicated. Be what you would like to see. It's not really "act until." Experience, be. You have no clue about the science—the science eludes you (and everyone). You can continue at an intuitive level and that's that! THAT is the real communication. You can put it into words, but your word symbols don't always mean the same thing to everybody. Just like your colors.

Anthony seemed to be struggling a bit here, casting about for the right words or analogies.

A: Anything you can see with the physicality, anything you can understand with the conscious mind has the potential to produce a negative and repel just like magnets. If you can put it into a concrete form, something like word symbols, or diagrams then it carries the potential—the potential to repel.

When you grasp something intuitively and you just embody it and display it, it is more neutral. It is more likely to produce an attractive potential. It is more likely to attract and therefore expand. You can teach and counsel and help and all those words, those supportive roles that attract you and yet repel you at the same time. You can accomplish what it is in how you view those roles that attracts you by embodying the intuitive messages you receive—those messages that contribute to your feeling joyful.

That really is what it is . . . enjoy. Be in joy! That is how you can most effectively bring your piece of the puzzle to heaven on Earth. It does not require orchestration, organization, systematization, structuring, or any of those activities on your part. You have had a love/hate relationship with those activities. You hold them closely and use them strictly in your own path. And you resist them strongly and avoid them purposely outside your path.

Duality, it does not fit. It rubs you the wrong way. You know that it takes you out of the flow. Step aside from it all. Let it wash out in that separator. Dispose of it. No, you really don't need to do anything. Just let it go. You don't have to sort it, pick through it, decide if it's good or bad, work hard to get rid of it, none of that. Just relax (sigh) *and let it go. Let it all just flow right out. Let it all just go. Just enjoy. Just enjoy. Just enjoy.*

Summary Notes:

The dishwasher has been a theme in our family for many years. It represents our need to do it right and showcases the differences in how we each see "right." Two dishwasher incidents came to mind as I read this transcript. If I search my memory I am sure there are many more, but these are the two that came immediately:

My son is seven years younger than my daughter. She went to a nearby boarding school for high school and then attended a university on the other side of the country. Since he was the only one at home for most of his growing up years, my son got the full benefit of our right/wrong training. At a very young age, he knew there was a right way to load the dishwasher. I taught him well. On Sundays, we had a big sit-down family dinner so the dishwasher would get pretty full. Our daughter would often be home for the weekend, and on this particular Sunday she was involved in the after dinner clean-up. When I walked into the kitchen after having driven my daughter back to school, my eight-year-old son was bent over the dishwasher, rearranging. He looked up at me with a rather disgusted look and said, "Can't you teach her to load the dishwasher properly?"

And more recently, my husband and I had "enjoyed a discussion" about the proper way to load our dishwasher in our house in Arizona. In this dishwasher, the cutlery goes into a series of containers running from front to back on the bottom rack. Since there were only two of us and we like to conserve water and power, we didn't run the dishwasher every day and the cutlery containers could get quite full. I spent lots of time in this house by myself and had developed the dishwasher system. I loaded the cutlery from back to front in an orderly fashion. When my husband would come down from Canada for a visit, he would load the cutlery from the front to the back. This bugged me. First it was not the "right" way, and second, I sometimes poked myself on the forks he put in the front when I was trying to do it right and put them in the back.

Because he was not there all the time, I let this slide, until one day when the stars didn't align and I said (rather nicely I thought), "I'm just wondering: why do you put the cutlery in the dishwasher starting at the front and working toward the back?" He replied (not so nicely, I thought), "I was wondering why you start at the back." Seems we both had our reasons; I did it my way so I wouldn't get stabbed, and he did it his way so the rollers on the bottom rack wouldn't get worn out pulling it in and out all the time.

Anthony knew that if he mentioned the dishwasher, it would be a fuller expression of the message.

Other than dishwasher silliness, this message for me is very profound. I highly recommend you read it several times. Let it sink in and become part of you. Embrace it.

Eighteenth Channel—March 16, 2013

This was an emotional day. My body was fatigued and my psyche was upset. I was alternating between lethargy, anger, and sadness. Part of me thinks this was integrating things coming in from the various sources I had tuned into in the last few days—Jennifer Hough's Blog Talk radio interview with William Linville, her *Quantum Wake Up Call,* and Oprah and Deepak Chopra's guided meditations. And part of me thinks it was because of the physically tiring few days I had just had. It didn't matter. It was uncomfortable and I was drawn to sit down in my quiet nest of pillows on the bedroom floor and contact Anthony.

My voice was very weak in this recording and in fact I wondered before I sat down to channel if my energy was high enough for Anthony to be able to use my voice.

IT'S YOUR MOVIE!

Paraphrased message:

Competition is a part of the life experience. Winning and losing are simply experiences. It is only judging them and being attached to an outcome that makes you feel bad. Wants are not something you have to think about or identify with your conscious mind. Wants come from your higher levels. They flow through your mind and are projected as your life. Assessing these wants, judging them and seeing how they fit with accepted roles and identities disrupts your enjoyment. Stop assessing and feel. Choose the wants that feel the best. Do not entertain those you do not want. Become attuned to what feels good. Feel it in your body. It can discern. Do not use your mind for discernment. Let your body talk.

The recording is 26 minutes long. At three minutes moaning started and I remember feeling as though words were being spoken but would not come out. The train floated in and out and I could clearly see the word *community*. Talking started at 4 minutes.

A: Yes, it's community, that's the word . . . the word you are seeing. It's community . . . communal . . . commune . . . oneness, with individuality. Community-unity—cohesiveness of purpose. Think of oneness with individuality, with cohesiveness of purpose, and the distinct lack of competition.

Here Anthony addresses one of the things about life that has caused me a lot of mind turmoil —competition.

A: Competition. That one's really got you, hasn't it? You think you should be able to win, to do better. And, then you think you sabotage yourself when you don't. Pretty wrapped up in that, got a good hold on it. *"It's just a game. I want to be the winner. Make it happen for me. It's not happening. Why didn't it happen? What is it? What is it? You wrote the script, you wrote the scene and it didn't play out. What is it? What is that? Is it an aversion to competition? Is it a judgment of competition? Is it an unwillingness to play the game? A desire to be collegial and yet unwilling to play the game? What is it?"*

Anthony is reiterating the questions I have asked and thoughts I have around competition.

It's nothing, really. It's an experience—either way, it's an experience . . . you win . . . you lose. Either way it's an experience. It's the dealing with it that's important. It's the recognizing that if I say I want to win then losing has been judged as being a lesser experience. Yes, I know, "So then why play the game? Why do it . . . to be collegial? To have some fun? To be part of a community? It's kind of a safe haven. We're all doing the same thing. We're all playing the same rules, using the same tools. It's kind of comfortable. It's enjoyable and yet it's not. Why do we do it?"

Why do cats play? Why do birds dance and sing? Why do coyotes howl? It's expression. It's an expression—an expression of how we feel, an expression of joy, an expression of 'I'm so happy.' "So why do we play the games? Is it really fun? Is it an excuse to be together? We'll create an organized sport or an organized game so then there is a reason for everybody to be together. We know what we are going to do, what we are supposed to do, and then around the edges we have fun. Is that what it is?" (Again reiterating my questions)

Community . . . communal . . . communing. How else can it be done? Is the need to have community, to be communal, and to commune a real, necessary, part of the life experience? Not necessarily. Humans do it in all different ways. Some choose to be hermits. Some choose to be street performers. Some choose to live in cities of millions. Some choose to live on remote farms —different ways. There is no right choice.

Anthony then switched to another topic. The question revolved around my questioning whether we needed to be part of a community, belong to clubs and groups, and to socialize with other members.

A: You have that question . . . that question about how sociable, how social you should be. It's all back to doing it right. Even when you know you can fly and you're free to be, do, to fly you feel the constraints . . . the constraints of societal rights and wrongs . . . the constraints of judgments, the pass/fail, the exams.

Know who you are. Know that if you just let go, put it on autopilot, set it for joy, you will go where you want to, need to, should . . . all of those words . . . go.

So then how do you occupy your mind? What do you think about if you're not assessing or planning or judging? How do you occupy your mind? What is the point? That's what you think. "If my mind were to be totally free from anything, I would be dead." That's what you think.

And now on to another of the topics that had occupied my mind for some time—wants.

A: Your mind is like a projector. The wants don't come from your mind. The wants come from our level. The wants come from our level through your mind and end up being projected on your screen of life—not by thinking, but by assessing and assigning feelings to the wants. Then you might think, "Well, is that a good thing? Is that really what I should do? How will it affect this? How will it affect that? I don't know how I feel about that." How you feel is uncertain. And what gets played on the screen is uncertain . . . a little bit of this . . . a little bit of that . . . some good shots . . . some bad shots . . . not really certain.

Change it around. Feel the wants. Feel the wants. They come in choices, bunches (here Anthony showed me a picture of a bouquet of flowers). *Pick the ones that feel good. Choose the wants that feel good and they will be displayed in beautiful living color on the screen of your life. Do not use your mind to search around for wants, to sift through them, to try and identify them, sort them out, assess them or grade them. NO. That only causes uncertainty, flickering, bumps.*

Just let the wants come, like a smorgasbord of possibilities presented in a beautiful array. Choose the ones that feel good and let your mind project them. Let your mind project them. Do not worry how they will be acted out, how the scenes come together, who the supporting actors are or where the props come from. Do not worry. Just choose the wants that feel good. Choose the wants that feel good. Do not assign grades or levels of want. Do not deal in "do not wants."

Practice. You will feel them. You will feel them. Pick the ones that feel the best. They are vague. They are not like words in your head or pictures. They're feelings. Become attuned to what feels good. Become attuned to your body. Sense it. Your body can give you the feedback at the time the want is sensed. Your body is receiving the options. Your body can discern. Do not use your mind for discernment. It cannot be used for discernment. The mind is not a receiver. The mind is not a transmitter. The mind is a projector. Let your body talk. Let your body talk. Let your body talk.

IT'S YOUR MOVIE!

Summary Notes:

In his message today, I believe Anthony was encouraging me to stop trying to use my mind to figure out what I want. He was asking me to just sense the guidance from my higher levels and use my body's messages to discern what was true higher level guidance and what was coming from my mind.

CHAPTER 17:
WEEK SIX

Nineteenth Channel—March 20, 2013

We were into the sixth week of this channeling experience and my life was definitely changing. Opening the channel and communing with my higher levels was now a very important part of my life. I could more easily discern higher level guidance from the chatter of my egoic mind and I was able to see energy as auras around people and objects and as patterns in the air.

The total time on the recorder was 28 minutes. During the first four minutes Anthony was preparing the channel, moving my eyeballs and mouth, and showing me visuals of the train, energy fields and veils. I also experienced energy jolts and tingles in my body. Anthony was telling me to open up and get bigger. I had the feeling of my body expanding like a balloon being blown up, and then there not being any demarcation between my body and the energy field around me. Anthony also told me there was lots of room in my body and he was in there with me some of the time. At the end, music was playing in my head. It was the Moody Blues song "Twilight Time." I hadn't heard this song for a long, long time.

Paraphrased message:

Games are meant to be played with enthusiasm. Enthusiasm is different from competition. Competition can create attachment to winning and losing and this attachment produces resistance and reduces your energy. The attachment also diminishes enthusiasm. Winning sparks enthusiasm and makes you want to play again, but if you win every time you also lose enthusiasm. Losing dampens enthusiasm. You become less enthusiastic with each loss. Winning and losing are just part of the game. Enjoy the game and move on. Do not become attached to winning or losing. He also cautions against getting caught up in things that start and end or worry about finishing something that no longer interests you just because you started it. Don't get locked into things with measurement and judgment. Do a variety of things. Be spontaneous, accept the results and move on.

Anthony began by singing softly.

A: *"It's twilight time . . . out of the mist, your voice is calling." You are getting much better at keeping your head out of the way, much more open and relaxed. You are still searching for the magic button—the magic button that opens up a new land.*

Here Anthony chuckled as he showed me a visual of a box opening and a new world appearing.

A: *The Promised Land—it's right there, right there in front of you. You can see it, you can. You see it around the trees. You see it on your screen. It's right there . . . right there for you to see, experience, love.*

Anthony was referring to the energy I can see.

A: You're getting the hang of it. You're quite surprised at that, aren't you? How you can jump and land on your feet in excitement and enthusiasm and not feel a thing.

I had been at a golf function the previous day where I was handing out awards and I let myself go, let the enthusiasm take me, not a prepared speech (this in itself being a new experience), just having fun. At two points, when I was handing out the big awards, I said, "Dat ta da da!" . . . and jumped up and landed on both feet with my arms extended—announcing the winners. This was surprising because I had seriously injured an ankle and the cast had not been off very long.

A: It's all it is, you know. It's all it is . . . enthusiasm—en theos—with God. Just jump, run, play, laugh. Yes, we are trying to get you to see that you are not bound by your timelines, by your years. How old are you, how old are they? No . . . that's not relevant. It's not helpful. It's not encouraging. You don't need that. The past, the present, and the future, they are all one . . . all the same.

I had a dream in the night, a vague dream of golf games and other games and then a message: "It's all the same—past, present, future. Change one and you change them all."

A: It's a bit confusing, that one, isn't it? Change the past—change the present. Change the present—change the future. Change the future—change the past—change the present. And around and around and around it goes. Just like those cups in the wind—around and around and around. Not back and forth—around and around and around. That's how the natural energy flows—around and around and around—not back and forth. Back and forth is like hitting a wall. Back and forth loses momentum, relies on other forces—gravitational pulls, outside influences ... around and around and around. The past—the present—the future ... around and around and around.

There is no timeline. Lines have a beginning and an end. There is no beginning—there is no end. Just around and around and around. You existed before you were created. There is no beginning—there is no end.

There is no winning—there is no losing—do you see? Do you see? Winning and losing is a beginning and an end. Enthusiasm goes around and around and around. And games, games are meant to produce enthusiasm. My team, your team—enthusiasm.

Enthusiasm is different from competition. You see children, they want to race. You let them win (chuckling). *They giggle and jump and you laugh with them ... enthusiasm. You beat them, you don't let them win ... they want to go again ... only this time they want to win. And if you don't let them, eventually they lose their enthusiasm for that game. The winning sparks enthusiasm. To keep playing and to never win kills enthusiasm, creates unhappiness ... creates competition ... creates "I'm going to win by making you lose" ... adds in new rules ... changes the game ... changes the starting point for some ... handicaps for others.*

Here Anthony showed me visuals of different starting points in a race for the less fast and the handicapping system used in amateur golf.

IT'S YOUR MOVIE!

A: . . . Changes the game. Spontaneous play . . . spontaneous games are played enthusiastically. Organized games. Organized play creates competition and rules. Organization changes the game because it lacks spontaneity. That's why you had so much enthusiasm, why you could jump without thinking about "How am I going to do this?" and land on your feet without worrying about "Will I hurt my ankle?" It was spontaneous. Spontaneity creates enthusiasm, en theos, with God. So how then do you play organized sports, organized games and maintain enthusiasm?

Here Anthony refers to notes I had written in my journal about winning and losing.

A: You felt it, you wanted to win big, and yet you felt "If I am able to win big every time, it kills my enthusiasm, and it kills their enthusiasm." You felt that. And yet you want to play better because you want to win. Winning sometimes maintains a degree of enthusiasm for all— dampened enthusiasm albeit, but enthusiasm nevertheless. And you can play against yourself to try and better your score, go farther, go faster . . . and it's the same thing. If every time you try you can go farther, go faster you are winning every time and you lose enthusiasm. There is no challenge. You know you can do it. The fun has gone out of it. It is the same experience over and over again. It becomes boring. You want to experience something new.

Acceptance. Acceptance is a big part of it. When you do not do better, go faster, go farther accept it. Yes, it is a similar experience if this happens every time, and then you lose enthusiasm. Variety, spontaneity, acceptance—the best of all worlds.

Yes, the quail are cute, the flowers are now beautiful, the birds are building nests. . . (chuckling) *and the bunnies are coming.*

Anthony shows me pictures and diverts my attention, as we do with children, when my mind starts to take over and analyze what I am hearing—and then he comes back to his message.

A: So much abundant life to watch . . . to enjoy . . . so much variety, abundance—it's all there. It's all there. The idea of "Stick to it, stay at until you get it, finish it if you start it"—it's all part of organization . . . grading, doing it right. There is so much there for you to enjoy, to experience—a whole world created for enjoyment and experience and creating. Do not get caught up in things that start and end. Find those that go around and around—bigger and bigger and bigger, creating, circling, loving, joyous experience. Join in—experience. Move on—experience. Expand—experience.

At this point, I was experiencing flying and zeroing in, seeing things on the ground very clearly and then flying on to the next thing.

A: Zero in—focus . . . see—really see . . . and then fly, fly, fly, fly . . . but not from here to there . . . not from start to end. Just fly . . . just fly.

Summary Notes:

Competition and the role it played in my life still occupied my mind. Anthony had tried to address it a few times but I was still not satisfied. Today he tried again. And it started to become clear for me. Although he said it before (more than once), it is the attachment to winning or losing, and the emotions we create that cause the discomfort. I think he is also trying to get me to stop beating my head against the wall to hit targets or win or finish things because I started them or maintain membership in clubs or social groups because I joined and it is expected. Or perhaps it was the way I looked at these activities that caused the problem.

Twentieth Channel—March 22, 2013

For several days I had been having visions of me as a sparkling bright pink star. This would happen during meditations and dream times. That morning I watched a YouTube video of a QHHT therapist describing a session with a woman who was a star seed from the planet Arcturus. This was the first time I had heard of this planet but the name really struck a cord so I went online to do some research. I was somewhat excited to see that Arcturus is sometimes referred to as the pink star. Here was something new for me to roll around in my mind. I asked Anthony about it, forgetting that he often brought these things out in formal channel sessions. I really wasn't ready for it, but out it came.

The total time of the recording was 35 minutes. Talking started after five minutes. We seemed to be having a bit of a mind tussle and when the talking started it was accompanied by groaning and gagging.

Paraphrased message:

The main message today, as I interpreted it, is this: "Your job is not to teach or lead or learn." I often envy those who channel beings or entities that have a message to share like Esther Hicks and Abraham or Lee Carroll and Kryon. That is not my path. "Your job is to own who you really are and just be. It is not to teach, convince, or lead. Your job is to see and be seen. You must learn to use your voice to be seen not to be heard."

Here are Anthony's words:

A: Yes . . . (groaning and gagging) Yes, it's why . . . yes, it's why . . . yes it's why. The idea of competition is so off-putting yet intriguing at the same time . . . it's why. It's why the pink . . . it's why.

Anthony is referring to the research I had done about Arcturus and Arcturians. I wanted to know if I was an Arcturian star seed and what it meant.

A: And you want to know "why" and "what" . . . "what does it mean to you really, now and here in this body and on this place . . . on Earth. What does it mean to you that you came from Arcturus? What does it mean? Why is it now? Why now do you know? Is it a comfort?" Yes, it can be.

I had been feeling quite powerful—almost overpowering.

A: You've been having these feelings of too much strength, too much power, different, forceful . . . force . . . powerful, unafraid . . . bouncing people off . . . people shying away . . . some not seeing, being attracted and some . . . bouncing away . . . being repelled . . . afraid . . . afraid. Sometimes you feel invisible . . . you are invisible. You go about your business. You interact . . . and not. It's like the turtle when he pulls his head in and has a nap. You're just pulling your head in and having a nap, taking a breather.

Anthony wasn't about to hold anything back that day. Now he brings up other visions I had seen where I was underwater.

IT'S YOUR MOVIE!

A: Yes, the underwater . . . that interests you too, doesn't it . . . fear on one hand and attraction on the other. You'll see . . . you'll see . . . new experiences . . . pushing the boundaries . . . enlarging the bubble . . . growing . . . expanding . . . freeing. You will see. Yes, competition really does have an interest for you doesn't it? It's something Arcturians do not experience. For, as you know it dampens energy. It is not forward and out. It is back and forth. Back and forth, not around and around and not forward and out. It is back and forth like a pickle ball . . . back and forth . . . back and forth . . . requiring the addition of energy at each back and forth. But not around and around and around like the big wheel in the water (visual of a grist mill) *going around, picking up the water, up over the top and back down again. Around and around and around . . . like the fan . . . around and around and around . . . in the wind* (visual of a windmill) *. . . in the water.*

I often wondered about electricity and if there wasn't a better way to use energy. I had done quite a bit of research on various methods and energy cycles and also on batteries and methods of storing energy.

A: Yes the electricity. The electricity is one that interests you also. The generation and the storage of power . . . ATP . . . ADP . . . ATP . . . ADP . . . requiring inputs. "How is it done without the wind, without the water, without the enzymes, without the catalyst—how is it done?" You have a remembering, a remembering that it is done. But that is a different world, a different frequency . . . one that cannot yet be replicated on Earth. You cannot yet teletransport, telecommunicate to the same degree as you remember. What you can do . . . what you can do is to experience with enthusiasm and to open up and allow . . . just allow . . . relax . . . float into it . . . float into it . . . experience where you are, where you have been, you will be again. Now you are where you are . . . in a world of generators and combustion . . . that is where you are.

Resisting dampens the energy . . . resisting stops your flow . . . resisting puts the brakes on. Take the brake off. Just let it go, let it go!

The emotions . . . the emotions are aids. The emotions can be helpful. They can provide a form of rudimentary guidance. They are easily interpreted messages. They are like . . . they are like turn signals, brake lights . . . they provide signals . . . signals for where you are going. Anger provides signals . . . a red face . . . balled fists . . . rapid, short breaths . . . signals . . . signals to those around and signals to the one experiencing. Emotions are a reaction to an experience.

Enthusiasm is proactive. Enthusiasm is a pre-emergent treatment for emotions. When you enter into an experience, a little bit of a new world—something new—an experience, with enthusiasm, you generate positive emotions.

Yes, I know . . . you wanted to know about Arcturus. You feel it. You feel it. You know the possibilities. You are not there. You are on Earth. Your job is to shift, to be, to help. Not with the physicalities, you're not here to help with the physicalities. You are here to be. And to be, you must take part. You cannot sit on the sidelines or stand in the dark and be. Just go. Just do.

It's hard for you, your voice . . . your voice is the one that causes you the most, the most concern . . . the most regret (blurting things out). *Learn to use your voice. Use it! Do not regret. Practice it! Use it! Not to call . . . not to lead . . . sort of as an announcer . . . an "I am here . . . I am here."*

As you withdraw from the Earth systems, the people systems that you were involved with (business, politics, social) *. . . that took your time . . . that provided you with the interaction, the socialization, what you saw* *as your life . . . the business, the competitive business . . .the learning, the education by research, by listening, by watching . . . the political system . . . the social structures. As you withdraw, there is a danger that you will stand in the shadows. That is why you must use your voice. Not to convince. Not to teach, but to say, "I am here." To say, "See me." . . ."I see you." . . ."See me." Not in the quilting bees, the ceramics classes, the golf clubs. Not in the political arenas, the business meetings. In the world! In the grocery store, in the seminars, in the world . . . like a comet . . . no boundaries . . . no borders . . . free to fly . . . free to be. "I am here." "I am me." "SEE ME." "I SEE YOU." "HEAR ME." "I HEAR YOU."*

Summary Notes:

Sometimes these channeling sessions are like pulling teeth. It seems as though nothing much is happening. It feels flat. I heeded the call to channel but was very tired and almost quit halfway through this message because I felt like we really didn't have a connection.

When I listened to the recording, I was tempted to just forget this one. Some parts of it were pretty far out there and I was concerned that the reader would be put off. Anthony did not agree. I was told that they are all important messages and they provide keys that will be built upon in conversations, videos and other communications and interactions. The message might seem disjointed or far-fetched, but it was to be included.

CHAPTER 18:
FINAL WEEK

Twenty-First and Final Channel—
March 31, 2013

This was one of our shortest sessions. The total time on the recorder is 19 minutes. Talking started after three minutes. During that time, Anthony was preparing the channel. I could feel him entering my body, working my mouth, expanding my chest; energy surged through my body, and then he was speaking to me internally, telling me to take my brain out and put it away. (This was an exercise Jennifer Hough taught us to do in the *Get Out of Your Own Way* course I had just completed.) I did as asked, mentally removing my brain and setting it on my lap, and then I saw the galaxies and stars. Anthony helped me to gather all the thoughts and pictures that were still floating around and to mentally place them in bubbles and watch them float away. He even had me send away the big white screen.

Paraphrased message:

Anthony was finished coaxing, cajoling, and jollying me. His message was serious and it was direct. "It is time to step into your true power and own it. It is time to stop seeking comfort and to let go of the ego. You don't need comfort or evidence. You are love, and love is all there is. You are complete. You are fully created. You do not need anything. Now is the time for creating and expanding upon creation."

A: *Thank you . . . thank you for clearing that all away. I have some things to tell you today that may not be answers to the questions that you are posing.*

As we were opening the channel, I was asking Anthony what I was supposed to do next.

A: *And so we have to keep it clear. The bubble idea is a good one. You can use that one. Just keep it clear because these . . . these are messages that require a clear, open channel. Clear and open. They do not relate to your childhood or to what you've seen and heard in this life on Earth. They relate to a much bigger, grander scale and they may not even be of comfort to you. Today that is not the goal. Comfort is not the goal today.*

You have been seeking a lot of that . . . comfort . . . cocoons . . . "Who's going to love me?" . . . comfort. It's time now to get over all that. It's time to expand your universe, your focus . . . locus. It's time. You have been traveling. Going to the stars, going to the center of the Earth, and to the ocean . . . seeking comfort. It is time to go beyond comfort. It is time to expand, to accept, to magnify, electrify, project. It is time. It is time. The ego needs to go. Step into it! Accept it! Get over it! No questions . . . bubble them (clearing my mind). *No metaphors.* (I love them.) *No comfort.*

IT'S YOUR MOVIE!

You do not need comforting. To seek comfort is to say, "I am in need of comfort." You don't need comfort! You don't need to keep it together, hold it in . . . you can't. You cannot. It will expand. You have given permission. You have accepted the role and it is now going to happen. It is now happening. It has now happened. You do not need to be comforted or to comfort.

There is no need for comfort. There is only love. You do not need to be comforted. It is now pouring through as your very being. Not through your being . . . as your being. It is thinning the lines . . . thinning the separation between your physical being and all that is. No! Put it in a bubble.

A thought had surfaced and Anthony wanted it out of the way.

A: You don't need evidence. Evidence is comfort. You do not need anything. You are love. Love is all there is. You are complete. You feel corralled or limited or harnessed when you forget that you are love. And you do not need to seek anything outside of you. You do not need comfort, evidence, support, attention. You do not even need experience. You are. You cannot be erased, humiliated, injured, shackled, killed, or ignored. You are. You are complete. You are done . . . not done as in finished or at the end . . . you are fully created. You are missing nothing. You do not need rebounded love energy to keep you going. You cannot be stopped. You do not need anything. You do not have to do anything. You are. You are. You are! THAT IS.

SECTION FOUR

Where To Next?

CHAPTER 19:

SIMPLE WAYS TO OPEN A CHANNEL

There is no magic formula, no secret process, no specialness, or right way of opening to channel. You need only a willingness to allow it and a readiness to lay down the need to manage, control, resist, or judge. As my beautiful friend Jennifer Hough says, there is only "Getting out of your own way!" It can be simple, but not necessarily easy.

Since you are reading this book, I know you are feeling the call, sensing your guidance levels in some way, wanting to know more, see more. Perhaps you would really like to be able to hear your guides and want to know how to go about learning to channel like I did.

I get it. We are living a human experience and as humans we like to have systems and processes. We seem to come preprogrammed with the need to know why, when, and how. We want answers. When will I achieve the success and abundance I want? When will I meet Mr. or Ms. perfect? What is the grand plan for my life on Earth? How long will I live? How can I lose weight or why do I gain weight? How can I make myself healthy or why am I unhealthy? And on and on . . .

If you are willing and ready to open your channel and communicate with your higher levels, you can easily do what I did—buy the book *Opening to Channel: How to Connect with Your Guide* written by Sanaya Roman and Duane Packer and follow the process they describe. You could also Google "learn to channel" and take advantage of the many different ways and teachings you will find. If neither of those routes resonates with you, I would suggest you try this process:

Read the transcripts of my formal channel sessions with Anthony. At first I thought they were pretty personal, that it was guidance and advice tailored for me and my unique (read special) life. Not so. Truth is truth. Truth might be transitory or evolving but there is always a truth. Toward the end of the formal sessions included in this book, Anthony made it clear that "he" is ME and when he speaks to me he is speaking to you and YOU. It is a concept we cannot quite grasp in 3D Earth terms. We appear to each other as individuals. We can get that we are connected. Some say we are all one, but these concepts don't quite do it. I can't describe it. I can only sense it.

Meditate. It matters not how you do this—it matters only that you do it. I used to think it impossible for me to meditate because I thought I had to empty my mind completely. I don't know if others can do this but it is not a possibility for me. I would go so far as to suggest that if you think your mind is empty, you are controlling it to the point that it is closed. What I mean by meditation is freeing your mind from judgment and preconceptions. It is simply allowing. I had very pleasurable meditation experiences when I participated in Oprah Winfrey and Deepak Chopra's 21 day meditation challenge last winter. I also enjoyed Deva Primal and Miten's chanting meditation series. Both were online and both were free. If you are not already a meditator, check out Oprah and Deepak or Deva and Primal or Google meditating and go with what appeals to you. However you choose to do it, do it! Don't worry about getting it right or choosing the right method. Just get started.

Meditate on the parts of Anthony's messages that "stick." When you read the transcripts, parts and pieces will stick in your mind or cause you to pause and consider something like, "I never thought of that," or "I never thought of it that way," or "I'm not sure I agree with that." You don't have to agree or disagree. In fact, it will help if you don't. Your higher levels will try harder to get through to explain or tell you your own truth. Just let those sticky bits roll around in your mind and meditate. When you do this, you will begin to see (in your mind's eye), hear, feel, or sense messages that relate to the sticky bits. Your channel is becoming unblocked. You are opening to the channel that connects you and YOU.

Make it a ceremony. Although there is no set process or way to "get it right" it does help to follow a guided process or have a little routine or ceremony, especially in the beginning. Your guides like this and it signals that there is clear intent on your part. It also helps to "get your head out of the way" and allows your guides to adjust frequencies to facilitate the connection. Your ceremony will be your ceremony; there is no right way, but I offer this as an example:

Choose a place where you will feel comfortable and safe. If you have crystals, feathers, or other important and meaningful items, place them nearby. Find a comfortable body position. Use cushions or a comfy chair—whatever feels best. You may be in this position for 30 minutes to an hour, so make it comfortable.

Choose a time when you will not be disturbed. Find a time when the house is quiet and unplug the phone if possible. You want your mind to be calm, relaxed, and willing, not on alert for family members or telephones.

Get your recorder ready. I use a relatively inexpensive little digital recorder with a small microphone that I clip to my shirt.

Now that you are in your "quiet place" with your recorder on, begin to consciously relax your body and quiet your mind. If you meditate regularly, follow your process. Or, follow this process:

Relax your body. Begin with your scalp. Feel the tension flowing out of your scalp. And now your face, feel any tightness or tension drain away. Your eyelids are starting to droop, and your breathing is becoming more regular. Feel your shoulders loosen up, as the relaxation flows down your arms and out through the tips of your fingers. Settle into your hips. Your back and your chest are now relaxed and the relaxed feeling is flowing down through your abdomen and on through your legs. Feel the relaxation flowing right out the bottoms of your feet.

Visualize an opening in the top of your head, your crown chakra. See a beautiful column of white light entering your body through your crown and flowing down through your head, down into your neck, through your chest, your abdomen, down through your thighs, the calves of your legs, and out through the bottoms of your feet. See this column of white light flowing out of your feet and down,

down, down into the center of the Earth. Watch the beautiful beam of light wrap itself around the core of the Earth and travel back up to your body. See it enter your body at the base of your spine and watch as it flows through all the bones and joints of your body. See them sparkle, beautiful white bones, and watch as the beam of light flows into your heart and out your body through your chest. See the light wrap around you like a beautiful cocoon. You are safe, you are protected, and you are open.

Repeat these words silently in your mind: "Mother/Father/God (you can substitute your own words to describe the one creative source if you like) I am now willing and open to accept divine guidance. Please help me to open and receive the truth of who I am. Help me to quiet my physicality and open to other dimensions. Help me release the need to judge or control. Release my fears and show me. I am ready now. Connect me to the highest level guide that is available to me at this time."

Then let it come. Go where it takes you.

Regardless of whether you get guidance and teaching through others, buy the book *Opening to Channel: How to Connect with Your Guide,* or follow the process I have outlined above, I urge you to do something. Take some steps and keep moving. In the words of Anthony: *Keep moving, and as you go farther you will see farther. You can't see there from here. Just keep moving!*

CHAPTER 20:

THATʼS A WRAP!

I have always thought of myself as being pretty black and white, process-oriented, and not all that creative. I wanted to be creative but never really thought I was. To me, creative people were musicians or painters. They were people who liked making crafts and projects. They invented things and decorated things and were not bothered by abrupt changes to plans or even the lack of a plan. They went with the flow.

My channel tells me otherwise. It tells me we are all creative beings. We all hold the potential to create. It was described to me in this way: *"The book encourages people to move forward, to step into the light, and create. It is 'beyond belief.' It goes beyond belief. It is like a light switch. You believe there will be light and when you go beyond belief—actually flip the switch—there is light. Energy has been used to create. It was untapped while isolated by the switch, but by closing the switch, it became available. Channeling is how you become YOU. Before you flip the switch and release the energy, it is merely potential. It waits.*

When I again asked how the book was going to help people, I was told, "*The greater audience, the audience for the book is searching. Find out what they are searching for. The answer remains the same. The answer is opening the channel, flipping the switch, making the connection. They are not sheep. They are interested and, for a bit, mesmerized by the messages they hear through professional channels. There is no proof—they hear different things and they search for* **their truth.** *They long to know who they really are, and what is there for them to do . . . how they can contribute in a meaningful way—beyond earning money, beyond impressing, beyond socializing, beyond being special. What can they do that will satisfy their own inner need? Not the needs of their peers, family, or neighbors—their own inner need—the need to CREATE.*"

One day, as I was pulling all my notes and files together, preparing the first draft that would be read by others, I heard this little laughing voice in my head: "*See—you are creative, you are knitting. You are knitting a book.*" Good one, Anthony. After I got over my fears and began to focus on creating my own movie, I realized how much I loved to write. It is my creative outlet. I still can't knit or paint or make crafts, but I can weave words. Fun!

I am not asking you to accept my truth. I am encouraging you to find your own. This is the purpose for publishing this book. As Anthony said to me in the beginning, "*Tell them the story. Show them that it doesn't have to be perfect, that you don't have to be a psychic medium or a professional channeler to connect with guidance levels. Let them see the messiness and hear the individual and personal way in which we communicate with you so they will be open to trying themselves and being excited by their own unique results. Encourage them to try to contact their own higher level guidance and to receive the loving messages and assistance in their own unique way, through their own unique filter, colored by their own unique life experience. We desperately want to communicate directly with everyone on Earth. Each is a sovereign, powerful, unique being, and we are waiting for them to open up to the possibilities so we can work directly with them."*

As we wrap up this book, I can see your guides and angels peering over the veil, urging you to connect, to accept your magnificence, and to release the judgment and resistance that have clogged your channel. They want you to step away from the roles and identities you have been supporting and protecting that no longer serve you. Own your power and stop seeking outside approval. YOU CAME INTO THIS EXPERIENCE PRE-APPROVED!

Perhaps you have already been receiving guidance but are unsure if it is real, or are concerned about how others might see you if you talk about your experiences. I believe this is why Anthony was so insistent on the "It's Your Movie" message. Write it the way you want to see it. If you are receiving guidance in some way and want to know if it is real or not, write, "I receive clear and loving guidance from my higher levels." See yourself that way and welcome what appears. See yourself as a person who can listen to leaders and teachers without judgment, taking what you like and leaving the rest. See yourself as neither a leader nor a follower. See yourself as the you that YOU want you to be. How others see you in their movie is beyond your control. Stay in your own theater. Write your movie as you want to see it play out. Write it for you, the only audience that counts and the only one there is. Write the theme, let it go, and then sit back, relax, and watch it unfold before your eyes.

You are a magnificent creative being. You are eternal and beyond harm in this life. It is YOU who decides when to leave your body and it is YOU that creates your life experience. YOU is calling on you to unblock the channel and allow what can be to be. Answer the call and reconnect with yourself. Allow yourself to create the life of your dreams.

POSTSCRIPT:

While this book was being processed for publication, Anthony urged me to write a companion workbook to assist those who are encouraged to open their own channel but are seeking more formal guidance than is included in this book. As with the book, I resisted but was told "Your role is to encourage AND assist. Write a guide to assist." And so I did. Information on where and how the companion guide, Everyday Channeling Guidebook, can be obtained is available at www.its-your-movie.com.